THE BATTLE OF BRITAIN

ROY CONYERS NESBIT

SUTTON PUBLISHING

First published in 2000 by
Sutton Publishing Limited · Phoenix Mill
Thrupp · Stroud · Gloucestershire · GL5 2BU

This paperback edition first published in 2004

British Library Cataloguing in Publication Data
A catalogue record for this book is available from the British Library.

ISBN 0-7509-3885-4

Typeset in 10/14 pt Sabon and 9/11 pt Gill Sans.
Typesetting and origination by Sutton Publishing Limited.
Printed and bound in England by J.H. Haynes & Co. Ltd, Sparkford.

By the same author

Woe to the Unwary

Torpedo Airmen

The Strike Wings

Target: Hitler's Oil (with Ronald C.
   Cooke)

Arctic Airmen (with Ernest Schofield)

Failed to Return

An Illustrated History of the RAF

RAF Records in the PRO (with Simon
   Fowler, Peter Elliott and Christina
   Goulter)

The Armed Rovers

Eyes of the RAF

The RAF in Camera 1903–1939

The RAF in Camera 1939–1945

The RAF in Camera 1945–1995

RAF Coastal Command in Action
   1939–1945

RAF: An Illustrated History from 1918

Britain's Rebel Air Force (with Dudley
   Cowderoy and Andrew Thomas)

The Flight of Rudolf Hess (with
   Georges Van Acker)

RAF in Action 1939–1945

The Battle of the Atlantic

Missing, Believed Killed

The Battle for Europe 1943–1945

CONTENTS

ACKNOWLEDGEMENTS

My thanks are due to all those who have helped with providing information or photographs for this book. They are Hugh Alexander of the Public Record Office, Rick Chapman in Germany, Knowler Edmonds, Peter Elliott of the Royal Air Force Museum, Jonathan Falconer of Sutton Publishing, Eunice Godfrey, Philip Jarrett, Mark Kirby, Paul Johnson of the Public Record Office, Colin Latham, Stuart Leslie, my brother Wallace A. Nesbit, Michael Oakey of *Aeroplane*, Graham R. Pitchfork MBE, Clive Richards of the Air Historical Branch (RAF), Jean-Louis Roba in Belgium, Bruce Robertson, Anne Stobbs, and Georges Van Acker in Belgium.

I am also most grateful to the artists who have provided paintings for the book: Roy Huxley GAvA, Mark Postlethwaite GAvA and Charles J. Thompson GAvA, ASAA, GMA, EAA.

Lastly, three friends have patiently checked the draft of my work and improved the narrative or the captions. These are Squadron Leader Dudley Cowderoy, Roger Hayward and Georges Van Acker.

CHAPTER ONE

THE ARCHITECT OF VICTORY

The British had fought many wars over the centuries, but almost all had been on foreign soil, some in distant parts of the world. In the First World War, though, Londoners and the residents of other British cities had a foretaste of things to come when Zeppelins and Gothas dropped bombs at night, causing indignation, then fury and even a certain amount of panic.

But the summer and autumn of 1940 were different. During daylight hours people in south-east England could see the conflict as it happened. White streaks of vapour high in the sky marked the paths of RAF and Luftwaffe fighters, while straighter trails indicated masses of enemy bombers heading inland. The concentrated rattle of machine-guns and the deeper thuds of 20mm cannons could be heard. Aircraft streaming flames and smoke plunged to the ground and exploded. The wrecks of RAF fighters were shielded from public view and cleared away quickly by maintenance units, but crashed Luftwaffe aircraft were left under guard for several days so that they could be seen and photographed by people who often cycled to the sites. If still in one piece, such enemy aircraft could be put on low loaders and displayed in town or city centres in order to boost morale.

Nights were spent in air raid shelters, while sirens wailed, bombs screamed down and then exploded, the ground shook, guns barked in an ever-growing chorus, and shards of hot metal from shells pattered down on roofs and streets. Mornings showed the grim results, with gaping holes in rows of houses, fires still ablaze and rubble choking the streets.

This was a time when almost all able-bodied youths and men had joined either the armed forces or part-time services, such as the Home Guard, the Observer Corps and the Auxiliary Fire Service, or became Air Raid Wardens or Fire Watchers. Many young women had volunteered for the Auxiliary Territorial Service, the Women's Auxiliary Air Service, the Women's Royal Naval Service, the Air Transport Auxiliary, the Land Army, the Auxiliary Ambulance Service or the nursing services, or were working in factories. Millions of older women spent their spare time in some voluntary capacity, unpaid and largely unrecognised.

The heroes of the hour were young men in air force blue, especially those who wore silver wings or brevets on their left breasts. Their strange new slang was entering the public vocabulary. Something easy was 'a piece of cake', a person killed had 'gone for a Burton', a crash was a 'prang', excellence was 'wizard', a crazy person was 'round the bend', an attractive young girl was a 'popsy' and a lengthy kiss with her was a 'snog'. Schoolboys idolised these young men, some of whom were little older than themselves, while schoolgirls adored them as white knights defending their country from the evil empire across the Channel. Parents and other relatives were filled with pride but justifiably fearful for the safety of their boys.

Air Commodore Hugh S. Dowding, photographed in 1922 when Chief of Staff of the RAF's Inland Area at Uxbridge in Middlesex. Born on 24 September 1882, he was then 40 years of age.

Bruce Robertson collection

The odds against the country seemed enormous. Looked at logically, from a weak and isolated military position, there seemed no possibility of defeating such an immensely powerful enemy, yet most people believed that somehow they would do so. Everyone was inspired by the grave words and timeless phrases of the Prime Minister, Winston Churchill, in speeches broadcast over the wireless which by then was in the home of almost every citizen. He called it 'their finest hour' and perhaps he was right. It was certainly a time of heightened emotions – exhilaration, determination, anguish, tiredness, self-sacrifice and fear. Those who lived through those months can never forget them.

The architect of the RAF's victory in the Battle of Britain was Air Chief Marshal Sir Hugh Caswell Tremenheere Dowding, the Air Officer Commanding-in-Chief of Fighter Command since its formation on 14 July 1936. Born on 24 April 1882, he was already past the normal retirement age in the RAF when the Second World War began, and in fact had been advised that he would be replaced in June 1939. However, his intended replacement, Air Vice-Marshal Christopher Courtney, was seriously injured in an air crash three days before the date of his appointment, and Dowding's tour of command was extended.

There was no doubt of Dowding's wealth of experience. Educated at Winchester, he attended the Royal Military Academy in 1899 and joined the Royal Garrison Artillery the following year, serving in Gibraltar, Ceylon and Hong Kong before transferring to the Mountain Artillery and spending six years in India. He then returned home to attend the Staff College at Camberley. He excelled at polo and skiing, and decided in 1913 that flying might further his career as well as offer an adventurous occupation akin to sport. After obtaining Royal Aero Club certificate no. 711 in a Vickers Farman 'Boxkite' at Brooklands on 20 December 1913, he underwent three months' instruction at the Central Flying School, Upavon, where he received his wings on the same day that he passed out from the Staff College. He then returned to the Royal Garrison Artillery but was placed on the reserve of the RFC.

Dowding was called up to the RFC on the day the First World War broke out, 4 August 1914, while still a captain. His first post was the command of a transit camp at Dover, where squadrons assembled on their way to France. On

5 October 1914 he was sent to 6 Squadron at Ostend, which was equipped with a variety of reconnaissance aircraft observing the German advance, and here he experienced anti-aircraft fire for the first time. The squadron retreated to France and in December he was posted as a flight commander with 9 Squadron at St Omer, which was developing wireless telegraphy for artillery spotting. The aircraft were dispersed to other squadrons in February 1915, but 9 Squadron was reformed on 1 April 1915 at Brooklands as a wireless training unit, where Dowding became a somewhat reluctant instructor.

This rather indistinct but rare photograph shows Major Hugh Dowding testing Royal Aircraft Factory BE9 serial 1700 in France in September 1916, when he commanded 16 Squadron at Bruay. The very strange prototype was a modified BE2c, with a tractor engine of 140hp moved aft and a nacelle in front in which the air observer sat. The whizzing propeller was between him and the pilot in the rear seat. He was armed with a machine-gun to give a forward field of fire, since at that time the synchronised gear which enabled machine-guns to fire through the propeller arc had not been perfected by the British. Major Dowding reported unfavourably on the performance of the aircraft and the danger to the observer. After further tests with 8 Squadron, the machine was sent back to Farnborough and further work on it was cancelled.

J.M. Bruce/S. Leslie collection

In July 1915 Major Dowding was posted to command 16 Squadron, based at La Gorgue in France and equipped with Maurice Farman and Royal Aircraft Factory BE2c reconnaissance aircraft. In the following January he was promoted to lieutenant-colonel and sent to the Administrative Wing at Farnborough.

Dowding returned to France in June 1916 to take command of the 9th Headquarters Wing at Fenvillers, consisting of 21, 27, 60 and 70 Squadrons, then engaged on strategic reconnaissance in preparation for the Battle of the Somme. Although not normally allowed to fly operationally, he received permission early the following month to lead a formation over enemy lines, with his adjutant as air observer. There was fierce opposition from German fighters and Dowding's hand was grazed by a bullet, but his observer was more seriously hit and they were forced to turn back. His squadrons suffered heavy casualties in the next few months and he fell out with Major-General Sir Hugh Trenchard, who commanded the whole of the RFC in France, when he recommended that they should be relieved periodically. This was construed as a sign of weakness by Trenchard, who called him a 'dismal Jimmy'. In January 1916 Dowding was sent back to England, as a full colonel commanding the Southern Training Brigade at Salisbury. He never returned to France but was promoted to brigadier-general in the summer of 1917 and awarded the CMG.

One of Dowding's obvious strengths was his ability as an administrator. His first appointment after the war was Group Commander at Kenley, with the rank of group captain, where he had the onerous task of organising the annual RAF Pageants. By 1921 he was in Uxbridge as Chief of Staff at Headquarters, Inland Area, with promotion to air commodore. In 1924 he went to Baghdad as Chief Staff Officer, Iraq Command. From 1926 to 1929 he was Director of Training at the Air Ministry. He then served from 1929 to 1930 as Air Officer Commanding-in-Chief of the Fighting Area, Air Defence of Great Britain. In the autumn of 1929 he was sent to Palestine, with the rank of air vice-marshal, to settle internal disturbances and came back with a very perceptive report. This met with the approval of the Chief of Air Staff, Marshal of the Royal Air Force Sir Hugh Trenchard.

He then served in the Air Council from 1930 to 1936 as Air Member for Supply, Research and Development, receiving his knighthood in 1933 and promotion to air marshal. In this period he insisted that RAF biplane fighters with wooden airframes be replaced by metal monoplanes with higher performance. The best fighter in 1934 was the Hawker Fury II biplane, armed with two Vickers machine-guns and with a maximum speed of 233mph at 15,000ft. Sydney Camm's Hawker Hurricane first flew in November 1935, to be followed by R.J. Mitchell's Supermarine Spitfire in March 1936. Both these new monoplanes were armed with eight Browning machine-guns and had top speeds more than one and a half times faster than the Fury.

In early March 1935 Dowding approved expenditure on setting up a station at Orfordness, where the Scientific Survey of Air Defence experimented with a system of detecting approaching aircraft with radio waves, as proposed by R.A. Watson Watt of the National Physical Laboratory. These early decisions by Dowding would eventually have momentous effects on the ability of the RAF to achieve victory in the Battle of Britain.

On 14 July 1936 the Air Defence of Great Britain, which was divided into the Western Area, the Central Area and the Fighting Area, ceased to exist. Instead, Bomber Command was created under Air Chief Marshal Sir John M. Steel, with Fighter Command under Air Marshal Sir Hugh C.T. Dowding. At the same time the RAF's Coastal Area, which had been formed as long ago as 15 September 1919, was renamed Coastal Command under Air Marshal Sir Arthur M. Longmore. Four days previously the RAF's Inland Area had been renamed Training Command under Air Marshal Sir Charles Burnett. Thus the whole of the RAF at home became organised on a functional instead of an area basis.

Dowding was not universally popular among his peers in the senior echelon of the RAF. This was partly the result of his personality. The high commanders in the RAF during this period had reached their positions from early careers in the First World War, when they had been notable for their courage, flying skill and general airmanship. They had also been lively and sociable members of the officers' messes when in junior positions. After achieving 'air rank', they were held in high regard but relied on their staffs to advise them and deal with some of the more mundane matters.

Dowding did not conform exactly to the norm. The nickname 'Stuffy' had stuck to him from his days in the army, for his somewhat austere and reserved manner. He was tall and lean, with a penetrating gaze. Although he was kindly in private life and had a quirkish sense of humour, he could be a caustic disciplinarian in his service career, intolerant of any shortcomings in others. He was capable of

The first flight of the prototype of Britain's best-loved aircraft, the legendary Supermarine Spitfire, took place on 6 March 1936. The airfield was Eastleigh, near Southampton, and the pilot was Captain J. 'Mutt' Summers, the chief test pilot of the parent company. Powered by a Rolls-Royce Merlin engine of 990hp with a two-bladed wooden propeller, serial K5054 performed superbly from the outset. Eight .303in machine-guns were fitted in December 1936, with 300 rounds per gun.

J. Falconer collection

The Gloster Gladiator, the last of the RAF's biplane fighters, first entered service in February 1937. These machines were on the strength of 3 Squadron at Kenley in Surrey, which was equipped with them from April 1937. Only 247 Squadron at Roborough in Devon flew Gladiators in the Battle of Britain, mainly in defence of the dockyards at Plymouth.
Philip Jarrett collection

delegation but expected first-class results from his staff and kept watch on every tiny detail of their activities. He was also a rather lonely widower. On 16 February 1918, at the age of 35, he had married Mrs Clarice Maud Vancourt (née Williams), a 27-year-old war widow with a small daughter. They had one child, Derek Hugh Tremenheere, born on 9 January 1919, but Clarice died tragically of appendicitis on 27 June 1920. Dowding was left to bring up the children on his own.

There was also the nature of Dowding's command, which had a primarily defensive role. This was a time when the main purpose of the RAF in Britain was assumed to be aggressive – the ability to knock out an adversary with its Bomber Command. Dowding's single-minded devotion to building up what was regarded as a secondary weapon did not appeal to all his peers. He became an Air Chief Marshal in January 1937, but was disappointed to learn that he had been passed over for the prized post of Chief of Air Staff. The incumbent, Air Chief Marshal Sir Edward Ellington, was succeeded by Air Chief Marshal Sir Cyril Newhall on 1 September 1937.

The technology which Dowding had fostered went ahead. His interest in Radio Direction-Finding (RDF) had been aroused on 26 February 1935 when a Handley Page Heyford of the Royal Aircraft Establishment followed the railway line between Daventry radio station and Wolverhampton, its track corresponding to the centre of Daventry's 50-metre beam broadcast by the BBC. Its presence showed up for most of the time on a cathode-ray oscillograph attached to a wireless receiver, proving that electro-magnetic energy from an aircraft could be depicted visually. From this beginning, apparatus in the experimental station at Orfordness on the Suffolk coast had been able to detect aircraft flying at about 25,000ft from distances of 25 miles or more. The stations emitted radio signals and the short pulses of energy bounced back from aircraft to the receiving towers. The results appeared as 'blips' on cathode-ray screens, with scales indicating distances.

In early 1936 work began on the construction of five RDF stations north and south of the Thames estuary. Their steel transmitter towers were 360ft high,

'THE FIRST STEP ...'
by Roy Huxley
An artist's impression of the scene over
Weedon in Northamptonshire on 26 February
1935 when a Handley Page Heyford from the
Royal Aircraft Establishment at Farnborough,
flown by Flight Lieutenant Robert S. Blucke,
made a low pass over a mobile laboratory
before climbing away to fly along the beam
between Daventry and Wolverhampton. Outside
the laboratory are Robert Watson Watt, the
director of the Radio Research Station at
Slough, and his assistant Arnold Wilkins.

Marconi Radar

transmitting at 10 to 13.5 metres, while the wooden receiver masts were 240ft high and received signals reflected from the aircraft. There were technical setbacks initially, but sanction for the completion of fifteen more of these stations was given in August 1937. These twenty stations, known as 'chain home' or CH stations, were rapidly erected around the south and east coasts of Britain, giving coverage of aircraft approaching at heights up to about 25,000ft.

However, further problems had to be overcome. One of these concerned low-flying aircraft, which the CH stations could not detect. For this purpose, 'chain home low' (CHL) stations were developed, with aerials set on gantries and transmitting on a wavelength of 1.5 metres. These rotated and searched for approaching aircraft, and had a range of about 100 miles. The first of these was not completed until 1 November 1939, but by July 1940 there were twenty-nine CHL and twenty-one CH stations. They stretched from the south-west tip of Wales and then along the south and east coasts of Britain up to the Shetland Islands. They were regarded as highly secret, although their tall masts were obvious to anyone in the vicinity. Operators were given warnings of dire consequences if they discussed their work with anyone outside their units. It was found that young aircraftwomen also became adept in this new class of 'radio operator', for which specialist training was required. (The term 'radar' was not

'THE SECOND STEP ... NATIONAL
DEFENCE'
by John Finch
The Chain Home RDF station at Ventnor in the
Isle of Wight, which operated from 1938 to
1961. It was the target for a determined attack
on 12 August 1940 by fifteen Junkers Ju88A-1s
of Kampfgeschwader 51 'Edelweiss', part of
Luftflotte 3. Most of the buildings were
destroyed, but a mobile station was brought in
while repairs took place.

Knowler Edmonds collection

used at this stage. This was an American derivation from 'Radio Direction And Ranging', adopted by the RAF in 1943.)

Another problem was how to distinguish RAF aircraft from the enemy with the apparatus in these new stations. This was solved by installing a device named 'Identification Friend or Foe' (IFF) in the aircraft, which produced a more prominent and different-shaped blip on the cathode-ray screen. Bomber pilots and their crews became wary of this device after the outbreak of war, since they assumed it enabled enemy night-fighters and flak batteries to detect their aircraft, and it became normal practice to switch on the IFF only when nearing the coast of Britain.

Yet another problem stemmed from the fact that all the RDF stations pointed seawards and had no coverage inland. Thus the Observer Corps, which had been created as early as 1924, was steadily expanded from four groups in 1935 to fifteen in 1939. By the beginning of the Second World War there were over 1,000 posts and 30,000 observers, covering most of the country. Almost all the observers were part-time volunteers trained in aircraft recognition. Many of the posts were situated in remote and bleak parts of the country. Their equipment consisted of an elementary theodolite, binoculars, a telephone and usually a small portable stove for making tea. The volunteers wore no uniform other than an armband and not all were highly proficient at first, although expertise developed steadily and the Corps gave superb service in the Battle of Britain.

Marshal of the Royal Air Force King George VI, attended by Wing Commander Edward Fielden (Captain of the King's Flight), carried out an inspection of RAF stations on 9 May 1938. His first visit was to RAF Northolt, where he was received by Air Chief Marshal Sir Cyril Newall (Chief of Air Staff) and Sir Hugh Dowding (Air Officer Commanding-in-Chief, Fighter Command) was presented, and where he inspected fighter squadrons. Then he moved on to RAF Harwell, where Air Chief Marshal Sir Edgar Ludlow-Hewitt (Air Officer Commanding-in-Chief, Bomber Command) was presented, and where he inspected bomber squadrons. Next, he inspected RAF Upavon, where Air Chief Marshal Sir Charles Burnett (Air Officer Commanding-in-Chief, Training Command) was presented and where he inspected the Central Flying School. His last call was to RAF Thorney Island, where Air Marshal Sir Frederick Bowhill (Air Officer Commanding-in-Chief, Coastal Command) was presented and where he inspected coastal aircraft. This photograph was taken as the King examined the Merlin II engine of a Hurricane I.

Aeroplane

Another essential part of the country's defences were the tethered balloons which protected cities, major towns, ports, docks and factories against low-flying aircraft. Balloon Command was created on 7 November 1938 under Air Vice-Marshal Owen T. Boyd and expanded rapidly. He was responsible to the Air Council for initial training and administration, but reported to Fighter Command for war training and day-to-day operations. This was another function to which aircraftwomen could be recruited.

Similar technical developments were taking place in Germany, where the scientists were equally advanced. What made them unique in Britain was the superb coordination in Fighter Command under Dowding. The nerve centre for this organisation was his headquarters at Bentley Priory, situated to the north-west of London at Stanmore in Middlesex. This mansion, purchased by the Air Ministry in 1926, had been the headquarters of the RAF's Fighting Area before the new commands were formed on 14 July 1936. When war became imminent, work began on installing an Operations Room and a Filter Room underground. This was not completed until 9 March 1940, when it became known to those who worked in it as 'the hole'.

The main purpose of this headquarters was to control all fighter squadrons in action. As with all other commands, Fighter Command was divided into groups. By the time the Battle of Britain began there were four of these, with No. 10 Group covering the south-west of Britain, No. 11 the south-east, No. 12 the centre and No. 13 the north. In turn, No. 10 Group was divided into two sectors, No. 11 into seven and No. 12 into six.

Fighter Command's headquarters at Bentley Priory, Stanmore in Middlesex, where reports from radar stations and the Observer Corps were received and incoming enemy aircraft were plotted on a huge board. Orders for interception were sent out to fighter groups which in turn passed them on to stations and then to squadrons. The procedure was extremely swift and effective.

Author's collection

The Filter Room at Bentley Priory was connected to all relevant units by an elaborate system of telecommunications set up by the General Post Office. Information fed into it, primarily from the RDF stations and the Observer Corps, was collated and analysed before passing to the adjoining Operations Room, from where instructions were passed on first to the various groups, then to the sectors and finally to the stations. This information was displayed on outline maps on tables, by aircraftwomen who received instructions through headphones and used magnetic rakes to move coloured and arrowed counters representing enemy and friendly aircraft formations. Of course, the controllers at Bentley Priory could not deal with detailed tactics. The 'scrambling' of fighters on the various airfields was controlled by the station commanders and their staffs in their own operations rooms, in combination with the various squadron commanders.

Fighter Command headquarters also controlled the operations of the Anti-Aircraft Command of the Royal Artillery with its gun batteries and searchlight formations. From July 1939 this was commanded by Lieutenant-General Sir Frederick Pile from his headquarters at Glenthorne, a house close by Bentley Priory. Dowding and Pile soon established a good working relationship, although the former was reserved and austere while the latter was genial and outgoing. They were both interested in technical matters and both pressed for more guns, searchlights and crews, for these numbers were insufficient for the defence of the United Kingdom.

Bentley Priory was responsible for the country's Air Raid Warning System, issuing 'yellow' warnings by telephone when enemy aircraft were within twenty minutes' flying time of districts ahead of them. Five minutes later, if the aircraft continued on the same track, 'Red' warnings were given and the ominous warning sirens were sounded. A 'Green' signal indicated that the raiders had passed, and then the sirens sounded the continuous note of the 'all clear'.

While Dowding was masterminding these developments, the RAF underwent a belated expansion. In 1934 the entire home-based RAF had consisted of only forty-two squadrons, at a time when Germany was building up her fleet to about a thousand front-line aircraft, in defiance of the Treaty of Versailles. In May 1935 Parliament had authorised an increase to 125 squadrons by March 1937, to achieve parity with this potential enemy. British manufacturing industry responded positively to this opening of the purse strings, but time was required to tool up and produce the new metal monoplanes. By September 1938, when Prime Minister Neville Chamberlain returned from Munich with a piece of paper which seemed to offer 'peace for our time', the squadrons of Fighter Command were equipped with only 93 Hurricanes and 563 outdated biplanes, although the first Spitfires were just beginning to arrive. This breathing space gave industry a chance to catch up. By the time war was declared, Fighter Command possessed over 500 modern monoplanes.

The expansion of the RAF required a great increase in airfields, and civil engineers were kept busy selecting sites and clearing them for runways and station buildings, mainly in East Anglia and Lincolnshire for Bomber Command. Existing airfields were upgraded to 'all-weather' status, with concrete runways and hard-standings. Recruitment was another problem, for almost two years were normally required to train a pilot to operational readiness and three years for skilled ground mechanics. The short-service commission had been devised for potential pilots by Trenchard as early as 1924. This form of recruitment was advertised in Britain and the Dominions, resulting in a flood of applicants.

The Royal Air Force Volunteer Reserve (RAFVR) was planned in 1936. This was the equivalent of the Territorial Army, whereby aircrew members could train in their spare time. It began in 1937 and proved immensely popular, with more applicants than the system could handle. Most of the pilots who flew in the Battle of Britain were young officers with short-service commissions or pre-war RAFVR sergeants, but there was a stream of others who had not completed their training. Training Command was so overstretched that plans were laid to begin aircrew training in the Dominions, under the new Empire Air Training Scheme.

War had become inevitable by this time, for Hitler had ignored the Munich Agreement, invading Bohemia and Moravia in March 1939. On 14 August 20-year-old Pilot Officer Derek H.T. Dowding joined 74 Squadron at Hornchurch in Essex, ready for flying duties in their Spitfire Is. Hitler surprised the world by agreeing to a 'non-aggression' pact with his greatest enemy, Soviet Russia, on 23 August. In conformity with his usual practice, this was worthless. It was merely a prelude to his invasion of Poland on 1 September, for the two dictatorships had agreed on how to share the spoils. On 3 September Chamberlain announced over the wireless that Hitler had failed to withdraw his forces from Poland and that in consequence Britain and France were at war with Germany. Half an hour later Fighter Command gave a warning and air raid sirens were sounded in south-east England, but the plotted aircraft turned out to be friendly and the welcome all-clear came twenty minutes later.

This type of two-seater biplane, the Maurice Farman S11 'Shorthorn', was flown by Captain Hugh Dowding in 6 Squadron at Ostend at the beginning of the First World War. It was powered by an 80hp de Dion pusher engine, with the air observer in the rear seat. This photograph was taken at an airfield in England during a visit by the Second-in-Command of the RFC, Lieutenant-Colonel Frederick H. Sykes, and the Deputy Director of Military Aeronautics, Major W. Sefton Brancker.

J.M. Bruce/S. Leslie collection

This Royal Aircraft Factory BE2c, serial 6195, is representative of the type flown by Major Hugh Dowding when he commanded 16 Squadron in France. Powered by a 90hp engine, it was built as a safe reconnaissance platform rather than for fighting, though it could carry two 112lb bombs. It became known as 'Stability Jane'. The pilot usually sat in the front seat. Some of these machines were fitted with a free-firing Lewis gun in the rear seat for the air observer.

J.M. Bruce/S.Leslie collection

This prototype of the Hawker Hurricane, serial K5083, made a successful maiden flight on 6 November 1935, fitted with a Rolls-Royce Merlin engine of 990hp. Production Hurricane Is were powered by the Merlin II engine of 1,030hp. Armed with eight .303in machine-guns, they first entered squadron service in December 1937 and became the senior partners of Spitfires in the Battle of Britain.
J. Falconer collection

Hurricane Is of 3 Squadron at RAF Kenley in Surrey on 23 May 1938. The squadron had converted from Gloster Gladiators to Hurricanes during the previous March. It reverted to its old machines in the following July while Kenley was extended to cope with monoplane fighters. Hurricanes arrived once more in May 1939 when the squadron was based at Biggin Hill in Kent.

Aeroplane

The Armstrong Whitworth Whitley was one of the RAF's heavy bombers after entering squadron service in March 1937. Some Whitleys continued with Bomber Command until April 1942 but meanwhile many were transferred to Coastal Command in the anti-shipping role. A few were converted to trainers for paratroopers, such as the example in this photograph.

Philip Jarrett collection

The Handley Page Hampden first entered squadron service in August 1938 as a fast twin-engined bomber capable of carrying a bomb-load of 4,000lb. The crew of four were rather cramped and the defensive armament proved insufficient for daylight raids, but Hampdens continued with Bomber Command until September 1942, when they were replaced by the new four-engined heavy bombers. This example was on the strength of 185 Squadron, based at Thornaby in Yorkshire on the outbreak of war.

Author's collection

Production of the Spitfire I began in 1937, with a Merlin II engine of 990hp and a tailwheel instead of the skid. Early aircraft retained the two-bladed fixed-pitch propeller, but the three-bladed variable-pitch propeller was introduced in the first production batch, as shown with K9942 here. RAF squadrons received deliveries from August 1939. Additional contracts were placed, making a total of 4,000 for the new fighter. This machine bears markings that were introduced after the Battle of Britain.

Author's collection

The first Spitfire Is were delivered in August 1938 to 19 Squadron in Cambridgeshire, as shown here.

Philip Jarrett collection

Pilots of 19 Squadron scrambling to their Spitfire Is at RAF Duxford in Cambridgeshire in May 1939, as part of an exercise.

Aeroplane

Ground mechanics receiving instruction on the Spitfire.

Aeroplane

This Hurricane I serial L1928 was badly damaged on 29 August 1939 at Biggin Hill in Kent when 3 Squadron practised night flying for the first time with monoplane fighters. The pilot was unhurt. The machine was repaired, as shown here, and entered service with 253 Squadron but crashed at Maidstone during a patrol on 10 October 1940, as a result of oxygen failure. The pilot was killed and the Hurricane smashed beyond repair.

Bruce Robertson collection

A Chain Home Low (CHL) rotating array, mounted on a gantry 20ft high.

Colin Latham collection

A group of Chain Home (CH) transmitter towers, 360ft high and made of steel. They are typical of those erected on the east coast of Britain.

Colin Latham collection

A group of Chain Home (CH) receiver towers, 240ft high and made of wood. They are typical of those erected on the east coast of Britain.

Colin Latham collection

'SQUADRON TURN'
by Charles J. Thompson
The artist's impression of the immensity of space, with a squadron of Spitfires almost lost against a background of storm clouds while creating a sweeping pattern.

The Filter Room at Fighter Command's headquarters at Bentley Priory. This underground block was opened on 9 March 1940 and became known as 'the hole'. The 'plotters' placed counters representing approaching enemy aircraft formations, including altitude and suggested strength, on the table as reports came in from various radar stations. On the right, outside the photograph, 'tellers' watched progress and informed the Operations Room next door, where the raids were plotted from reports which came in from Royal Observers Corps posts after the enemy had crossed the coast. The Operations Room issued orders to defending RAF stations, which vectored their aircraft on to the enemy aircraft.

Flight Officer Felicity Ashbee WAAF

The Observer Corps was formed in 1924 and was steadily increased in the interwar years. It became an essential part of Britain's defences during the Battle of Britain, with posts covering the entire country.

Author's collection

A post manned by volunteers of the Royal Observer Corps, equipped with binoculars and theodolite. England, Wales and Scotland were covered with these posts during the Second World War.

Author's collection

One of the Royal Observer Corps centres at work. Information from the network of posts in the neighbourhood was passed by direct telephone line to the centre. The course, height and identity of every aircraft, both hostile and friendly, was plotted on the operations table. From each centre, information was passed to the headquarters of the Fighter Command Group in the area.

Author's collection

This propaganda photograph of the Heinkel He100D-1 represents a hoax. The machine was a variant of the He100V-2 in which Ernst Udet established a new world speed record on 6 June 1938 of 394.4mph at 18,000ft on a 100km circuit. Twelve of these He100D-1s were fitted with a 20mm cannon and two MG17 machine-guns, sprayed in standard Luftwaffe finish with fictitious unit markings such as the lightning flash shown here, and designated as a new He113 fighter. These twelve aircraft were resprayed periodically, giving the impression that a large number were in service. They were never encountered in combat, for the Luftwaffe was satisfied with its Messerschmitt Bf109 fighter.

Philip Jarrett collection

Messerschmitt Bf109V (for Versuchsnummer or experimental number) 20, coded CE+BM and flown by the test pilot Dr Hermann Wurster. This was the eighth experimental aircraft before the Bf109E-3 went into production and became the most important sub-type of the 'Emil' engaged in the Battle of Britain. It had a better rate of climb and dive than either the Spitfire or the Hurricane but could not turn in such a tight circle.

Philip Jarrett collection

CHAPTER TWO

INVASION

On the outbreak of the Second World War Fighter Command consisted of thirty-nine squadrons, although fifty-two were considered the minimum necessary for the defence of the United Kingdom. It had been agreed that Fighter Command should be expanded, with seven new squadrons to be formed within six months and twenty more by April 1941. This huge increase was under way, and Air Chief Marshal Sir Hugh Dowding was certainly anxious to build up his defensive force. In the meantime the numbers were depleted with the despatch of four Hurricane squadrons to France as part of the Air Component of General Lord Gort's British Expeditionary Force. Six more Hurricane squadrons were put on a mobile footing in case they were needed later.

The remainder of this Air Component consisted of five squadrons of Westland Lysanders and five of Bristol Blenheims, for tactical support. Ten squadrons of Fairey Battles formed the RAF's Advanced Air Striking Force in France. These two RAF arms, known as the British Air Forces in France, were under the command of Air Marshal Sir Arthur S. Barratt. They could not be described as formidable, and reliance had to be placed on the French Air Force.

Although the Fairey Battle entered squadron service in May 1937, it was already obsolescent when the Second World War broke out. Intended as a light bomber for tactical work, carrying 1,000lb of bombs and armed with two machine-guns, it proved no match for German fighters when the Blitz began in the west. Most of the remaining Battles were turned over to training duties in 1940.

Author's collection

Meanwhile the British estimate of the Luftwaffe's strength proved to be somewhat exaggerated. This belief had stemmed partly from the German Propaganda Ministry, which gave the impression that about 1,650 front-line bombers were available. The figure was in fact 1,180 twin-engined bombers, of which 1,008 were serviceable. Nevertheless the Luftwaffe was extremely powerful, with 4,161 aircraft of all types, including transport. The RAF in Britain and France, together with the French Air Force, mustered a total of 3,695 front-line aircraft, but large numbers of these were obsolescent.

Almost all the operational units in the Luftwaffe served in four Luftflotten, or air fleets. Each fleet had its own bomber, fighter, ground-attack, reconnaissance and other units, all trained to operate in close tactical support with the various armies. Luftflotte 1 covered the north and east of Germany, under General der Flieger Albert Kesselring. Luftflotte 2, under General der Flieger Hellmuth Felmy, covered the north-west. Luftflotte 3, under General der Flieger Hugo Sperrle, covered the south-west. Luftflotte 4, under General der Flieger Alois Loehr,

A pilot climbing into the cockpit of a Messerschmitt Bf109E-1 of I./Jagdgeschwader 20, after the mechanic had started the engine. This unit participated in exercises in June 1939 in preparation for the attack on Poland. It was redesignated III./Jagdgeschwader 51 on 4 August 1940.

Philip Jarrett collection

covered the south-east. These four air fleets were far more suited to fight a land war than either the RAF or the French Air Force.

The term 'phoney war' which was given to the first eight months from September 1939 did not apply to Poland. That country experienced the new Blitzkrieg tactics when forty-eight German divisions attacked on 1 September, with their Junkers Ju87 Stukas blasting a path ahead of rapidly moving armoured columns. Most of the aircraft in the Polish Air Force were obsolete, and Luftflotten 1 and 4 destroyed almost all of them on the ground in the first few days. The Polish army resisted bitterly but was overwhelmed. On 17 September Russian forces invaded the country from the east. The Luftwaffe had no hesitation in bombing Warsaw on 25 September, and Poland capitulated two days later, to be partitioned by two vicious dictatorships. The Luftwaffe lost 285 aircraft, with 279 others damaged, during this campaign.

In the west both sides refrained from bombing targets where civilian casualties would be high. Of course military targets were considered legitimate, and for the most part attacks were confined to naval vessels. Bomber Command's belief in the effectiveness of its aircraft operating in close formation, protected by combined fire from their power-operated turrets, was shattered when squadrons sent out in daylight suffered heavy casualties from enemy fighters. Its activities were soon restricted mainly to dropping leaflets over Germany at night, with no effect on the determination of the enemy to wage war. Coastal Command soldiered on with aircraft of limited performance and numbers, patrolling the seas and protecting convoys.

Fighter Command also patrolled the coasts of Britain, in attempts to intercept enemy reconnaissance and mine-laying aircraft, but its control system suffered a humiliating blow when two RAF formations were brought into combat with each other. This began in the early morning of 6 September 1939 after a searchlight battery reported aircraft at high altitude over West Mersea in Essex. Air raid sirens were sounded and RAF North Weald despatched twelve Hurricanes from 56 and 151 Squadrons to intercept what appeared to be a hostile force. Two other pilots of 56 Squadron took off soon afterwards to join in the chase. Then twelve Spitfires of 74 Squadron plus two flights from 54 and 65 Squadrons were ordered off from Hornchurch in Essex.

The formations of Hurricanes and Spitfires were vectored on to each other west of Ipswich. There was bright sunshine and from a distance the Spitfire pilots had difficulty in making positive identifications. Three Spitfires of 74 Squadron dived on the two Hurricanes of 56 Squadron which had taken off after the main formation. Two of these Spitfires opened fire and a Hurricane went down, the pilot killed by a bullet in the head. The other Hurricane was hit but the pilot made a forced landing and was unhurt. All the other fighters whirled about in the sky but fortunately did not open fire. But itchy-fingered anti-aircraft gunners opened fire and another Hurricane was damaged, although the pilot was unhurt.

This tragic fiasco was kept secret from the public but caused fury in Fighter Command headquarters, where it was handled by Air Vice-Marshal Keith Park, Senior Air Staff Officer (SASO) to Dowding at the time. The three Spitfire pilots were arrested and one of the sector controllers was removed from his post. All the reporting procedures in Fighter Command and its dependent units were tightened up and regularised, including the 'telling' methods at Bentley Priory.

So the war continued, while a strange calm persisted over the battle front. Hitler still hoped to conclude a peace with Britain and France, but in any event the Wehrmacht needed to build up its strength for future attacks. At the same time, the eight months of remission gave the Fighter Command an opportunity to improve its effectiveness. More monoplanes were produced and the essential CHL stations were built. The plan for expansion went ahead, and indeed eighteen new squadrons were formed by the end of 1939, although not all were at operational readiness. Training of both groundcrews and aircrews was accelerated, with new facilities for the latter being opened in Canada and Southern Rhodesia.

The far-seeing Dowding allowed two of his precious Spitfires, serials N3071 and N3069, to be diverted on 30 October 1939 from Maintenance Command to the new Heston Flight, a unit which would eventually become the Photographic Development Unit and supply British Intelligence with superb visual information. He lost two more of his squadrons on 15 November 1939 when they were sent to France. These were Auxiliary Air Force squadrons, equipped with Gladiator biplanes, although they converted on to Hurricanes in time for the Battle of France.

In this 'phoney war' period, the Government Code and Cypher School at Bletchley Park in Buckinghamshire was working on ways to break the seemingly impenetrable 'Enigma' codes used by the Germans. It had begun to decrypt those used by the Army and the Luftwaffe by the time Hitler made his next move. This was his invasion of Denmark and Norway on 9 April 1940, ostensibly to protect the passage of high-grade iron ore being supplied by Sweden via Norway to feed his war machine. The build-up of German invasion forces had been known to the British, who did their best to hinder the Kriegsmarine by laying mines in Norwegian waters and hunting for the seaborne invasion forces. However, nothing could be done to prevent the Wehrmacht moving into Denmark, a country which was unable to defend itself against such might.

Under Operation Weserübung, Fliegerkorps X, commanded by Generalleutnant Hans Geisler, committed about 100 fighters and 320 bombers for the assault on Norway, supported by about 500 transports carrying paratroopers and other airborne soldiers. The Norwegians fought desperately and were backed by British contingents which landed at Namsos and near

The Dewoitine D520 was the best and most elegant fighter in the French Air Force, but it did not begin to reach the squadrons until May 1940. Powered by a Hispano-Suiza 12Y-45 engine of 910hp, it had a maximum speed of about 330mph. It was armed with one Hispano-Suiza 20mm cannon and four 7.5mm machine-guns. These fighters saw some action before the fall of France. Production continued under German control and some machines were allocated to Italy, Bulgaria and Romania, while the Luftwaffe employed others as trainers.

Gaston Botquin collection via Jean-Louis Roba

Fifteen Gloster Gladiator Is were on the strength of the Belgian Air Force on 10 May 1940, including serial G-23 of the 1st Squadron, 1st Group, 2nd Aeronautical Regiment. Each was powered by a Bristol Mercury engine of 840hp and fitted with four 7.65mm machine-guns, two beneath the wings and two on the fuselage. Six took off on 11 May to protect the RAF's Fairey Battles detailed to attack the bridges over the Albert Canal. They were attacked by Messerschmitt Bf109s near their objective. Three were destroyed and three others were damaged and made forced landings. The other nine Gladiators were either shot down or destroyed on the ground within the first two days of the Blitzkrieg.

Georges Van Acker collection

Narvik on 14 April, followed by more at Andalsnes. Air cover was provided by carrier-borne aircraft of the Fleet Air Arm. On 24 April eighteen Gladiators of Fighter Command's 263 Squadron landed from the carrier HMS *Glorious* on the frozen Lake Lesjaskog, near Andalsnes. The result was disastrous. The severe cold froze carburettors and controls overnight, so that only four were able to take off again. Relays of German bombers arrived and by the following evening all save five Gladiators had been destroyed. The squadron made one last effort, until only one aircraft remained serviceable. The pilots were then withdrawn by sea. By the end of the month, the British forces in central Norway, at Andalsnes and Namsos, were also pulled out.

The British contingents at Narvik were reinforced, and fighting was continuing when the Wehrmacht struck in the west, on 10 May, under Operation Fall Gelb (Case Yellow). This move had also been anticipated by the Anglo-French forces and the British Expeditionary Force moved into Belgium to counter the initial thrust through the Low Countries. The four Hurricane squadrons in England under the reinforcement plan flew to France to join the six squadrons already there. Two others were scheduled to go to Norway, leaving Dowding with forty-one squadrons for home defence, compared with the agreed minimum requirement of fifty-two.

The German forces for the invasion of the Netherlands, Belgium and France consisted of 157 divisions, backed by 1,148 bombers, 1,264 fighters, 640 reconnaissance and 475 transport aircraft. The combined Allied forces totalled 135 divisions, including the Belgian and the Dutch. Many of the French divisions were formed from unwilling and poorly trained conscripts. The Germans were overwhelmingly superior in the air. There were only about 400 RAF aircraft of all types in France. Further south, the French Air Force consisted of about 1,450 aircraft, of which about half were obsolete, and its squadrons were seriously short of trained aircrews.

Luftflotte 2 under General der Flieger Albert Kesselring supported Army Group B under Generaloberst Fedor von Bock in the north, while Luftflotte 3 under General der Flieger Hugo Sperrle struck French positions around Sedan near the River Maas. Airfields and towns in the Netherlands, Belgium and northern France were raided, while airborne troops occupied bridges across the Maas estuary. The Royal Netherlands Air Force possessed about 130 aircraft and fought bravely before being overwhelmed, causing heavy casualties among Luftwaffe units. The Belgian Air Force had about 150 obsolete biplanes, mostly devoted to reconnaissance, plus 11 Hurricanes and 14 Battles. In the first two days the Luftwaffe destroyed 110 of these aircraft, while the Belgian aircrews fought heroically, even suicidally, against impossible odds.

Three Panzer Corps attacked at speed through the Ardennes forest in south Belgium, an area which had been considered impractical by the Allies, and punched a gap between the British and French divisions. The Blitzkrieg tactics worked once more, with Stukas blasting pockets of resistance in front of armoured columns and infantry, which then cut off army formations. The Allied armies had little effective response to these air attacks, but they fought on. By 14 May Dutch resistance so angered Hitler that he ordered the bombing of Rotterdam, causing great devastation and heavy civilian casualties. The country had no option but to surrender the next day.

Meanwhile the RAF bombers tried to stem the German advance through Belgium but were shot down by mobile flak units or fighters. Of the 135 Battles and Blenheims in France, almost half were lost in the first three days, and forty more the following day. With the RAF's Advanced Air Striking Force virtually wiped out, there was no air power left to halt the German spearheads. The Hurricane squadrons also acquitted themselves gallantly, destroying many Luftwaffe aircraft, but they were too few in number. Within four days of fighting the ten squadrons lost over half their strength. The RAF possessed some mobile RDF stations but the speed of the Wehrmacht disorganised these. The reconnaissance Lysanders could do little in skies dominated by the Luftwaffe.

The Avions Fairey Firefly was built for the Belgian Air Force, adapted from the Fairey IIM intended for the RAF but rejected in favour of the Hawker Fury which first flew in March 1931. It was powered by the Rolls-Royce Kestrel IIS engine of 480hp, fitted with two forward-firing machine-guns, and had a top speed of 223mph at 13,000ft. Most were built under licence at Gosselies in Belgium. This Firefly II serial Y-76 was photographed at Nivelles airfield when on the strength of the 3rd Squadron, 2nd Group, 2nd Aeronautical Regiment. Although the pride of the Belgian Air Force in their day, these machines were obsolete during the Blitzkrieg. Their only action was on 14 May 1940 when ten were ordered to fly over Belgian troops to boost their morale. One was shot down by Belgian artillery. The others flew south and arrived at Montpellier in France on 20 May, where they were used as training aircraft. They ended their career in North Africa.

Georges Van Acker collection

In Britain Neville Chamberlain had resigned and a new National Government formed under Winston Churchill on 11 May. Two days later the Air Ministry ordered Dowding to send thirty-two Hurricanes (equivalent to two full squadrons) to France in response to an urgent request from the military. These were drawn from a number of squadrons and duly sent. On the following day the French Premier, Paul Reynaud, appealed for ten more RAF fighter squadrons to be sent over the Channel to support the French line, already crumbling on the River Meuse. On hearing this, Dowding stated at a Cabinet meeting on 15 May, 'If the present rate of wastage continues for another fortnight, we shall not have a single Hurricane left in France *or* in this country.' Reynaud's request was rejected and instead sanction was given for Bomber Command to make its first strategic bombing attack on German industry. Ninety-nine aircraft were despatched that night against targets in the Ruhr. However, Dowding was ordered on the next day to supply eight half-squadrons of Hurricanes for operations in France. By then, his force in the UK was reduced to the equivalent of about thirty-six squadrons, taking into account replacements. Churchill visited France on that day and was filled with such dismay at the plight of the country that he telegraphed asking for six more squadrons. By then, the airfields in France were being overrun, and these extra squadrons operated from Kent.

On 16 May Dowding expressed his deep concern in a letter to the Under-Secretary of State at the Air Ministry. He pointed out that the Air Council had estimated that the force necessary to defend the country was fifty-two squadrons, but he had only thirty-six available. If any of these were sent to France they would suffer heavy losses. He wished to know how many squadrons were to be kept at home and remarked that if his defence force was drained away in desperate attempts to remedy the situation in France, this would result in 'the final, complete and irredeemable defeat of this country'.

Three days later Churchill ruled that no more squadrons should be sent to France. In any event the situation had become so impossible that those aircraft fighting in the doomed country were beginning to return home, to operate over the battlefield from more distant but safer airfields. On the same day Lord Gort warned that his forces north of the Somme were under such pressure that a withdrawal to England via Dunkirk could be necessary.

Fighter Command and the squadrons in France were not left to fight on their own. Bomber Command had been active against the enemy from 10 May, and it did all it could to provide support to the retreating British Expeditionary Force in this desperate period. It sent 122 heavy aircraft to bomb enemy communications around the battle front on the night of 23/24 May, 69 Blenheims against German positions near Calais on 24 May, 59 heavy bombers against communications on the night of 24/25 May, 42 Blenheims against bridges and transport on 25 May, and 103 heavy bombers against troop positions and communications on the night of 25/26 May.

The Vickers Wellington was Bomber Command's standard heavy bomber during the Battle of Britain, engaged on raids over Germany and targets in the occupied countries. First introduced into squadron service in October 1938, it was a reliable aircraft, heavily armed and capable of a range of 1,200 miles with 4,500lb of bombs. These Wellington Is were on the strength of 9 Squadron at Honington in Suffolk, a squadron which shared in the first attack made by Bomber Command, against German warships at Brunsbüttel on 4 September 1939.

Author's collection

Boulton Paul Defiant I, serial L7012, without machine-guns in the turret, from the first production batch of eighty-seven aircraft. The first to receive these machines, in December 1939, was 264 Squadron, when based at Martlesham Heath in Suffolk.

Philip Jarrett collection

The main evacuation from Dunkirk began on 26 May, covered by fighters operating from airfields in the south-east of England. Tactical control of this coverage fell to the Air Officer Commanding No. 11 Group in the south-east of England, Air Vice-Marshal Keith Park, who until a few weeks before had been Senior Air Staff Officer (SASO) to Dowding. Park was a fighter pilot with enormous experience dating back to the First World War, and in combination with Dowding he deployed his squadrons with great skill. Sixteen squadrons were available, operating on 27 May in single squadron strength, two squadron strength on the following day, and four squadron strength thereafter. The pilots sometimes flew three operations a day. It was impossible to increase the number of squadrons without denuding other parts of the country of its air defence.

Hurricanes, Spitfires and Defiants were employed, the latter enjoying considerable success initially until the Luftwaffe pilots learnt that its armament fired rearwards and upwards but not forwards. The Hurricanes and Spitfires proved equal matches for the Messerschmitt Bf109 single-engined fighter, superior to the Messerschmitt Bf110 twin-engined fighter, and devastatingly effective against the Junkers Ju87 dive-bomber. Heinkel He111s received rough treatment whenever they appeared. Bomber Command continued its operations, with the heavier bombers operating at night and the Blenheims during daylight.

Most of these air combats took place out of sight of the troops on the beaches, who had no shelter and little defence apart from rifles against air attack. Inevitably, some Luftwaffe aircraft got through and the men suffered the appalling experience of being bombed and strafed in the open. The belief grew that the RAF had deserted them in their desperate hour of need, and for weeks afterwards the junior service was in bad odour with the rank and file of the army. The truth was that Fighter Command lost over a hundred aircraft in the evacuation from Dunkirk, from which only about twenty pilots were rescued. It destroyed about 130 enemy aircraft in that period. Over 224,000 officers and

A Junkers Ju87B-2 of 4./Sturzkampfgeschwader 2, photographed in 1940. This machine was capable of diving at an angle of about 80 degrees and had a maximum speed of about 350mph. It pulled out automatically when the pilot pressed a button on his control column and the bomb was released. A wind-driven 'screamer' was fitted, to terrify those below. This dive-bomber became detested by British and French troops in France but stood little chance against Spitfire and Hurricane pilots in the Battle of Britain, being especially vulnerable to attack after pulling out of its dive.

Philip Jarrett collection

men were brought over the Channel by the Royal Navy and the armada of small ships which sailed from England, and eventually about 114,000 more came to England from ports further west. On 23 May Hermann Goering had boasted to Hitler that the Luftwaffe alone could wipe out these forces. In this, as in many other matters, he was proved wrong.

This evacuation sealed the fate of France but fighting continued for several weeks. Italy made an inglorious move by invading the country on 10 June. France capitulated on 22 June, when the country was dismembered into two zones, the north and west under German control and the remainder nominally ruled from Vichy under Marshal Henri P.O. Pétain. Meanwhile Dowding lost most of another squadron when the British forces were evacuated from Norway and the Hurricanes of 46 Squadron landed on the deck of HMS *Glorious*; this aircraft carrier was sunk with almost all on board south-west of Narvik on 8 June.

With France crushed, Hitler hoped that Britain would be prepared to make peace and perhaps even join in his intended attack on Soviet Russia, planned for the following year. When his overtures were contemptuously rejected by Churchill, plans for the invasion of England were drawn up, under Operation Sealion. The German High Command first contemplated a series of landings stretching from Ramsgate in Kent to Lyme Regis in Dorset, with troops provided by the victorious Army Group A under Field Marshal Gerd von Rundstedt and Army Group B under Field Marshal Fedor von Bock. The whole enterprise was under the direction of the Commander-in-Chief of the Army, Field Marshal Walther von Brauchitsch. A vast training programme began in the last week of July. Thirteen divisions were sent to northern France and each split into two echelons for the invasion. The first echelons of about 7,000 men apiece were equipped with tanks, armoured vehicles, mountain guns, machine-guns, mortars, anti-tank guns, anti-aircraft batteries, bicycles and horses. The second echelons, of about 12,000 men apiece, would bring more tanks and heavy weapons. Thus about 250,000 men were committed to the invasion, together with a huge amount of equipment.

The problem was how to convey this great force over the 'extended river crossing', as it was called. Admiral Erich Raeder of the Kriegsmarine dismissed the original plan as impractical but at a conference with Hitler on 31 July said that it could be done on a much narrower front. The main proviso was whether the Luftwaffe could establish complete air superiority over the RAF. Hitler duly ordered the Luftwaffe to do so as soon as possible and the Army to continue its preparations.

Raeder began to collect all the shipping available – merchant ships, trawlers, barges, tugs and motor-boats – by withdrawing them from their normal occupations in France, Belgium and the Netherlands. The German High Command decided that the main landings would take place on two shorter strips of coast, from Folkestone to New Romney in Kent and from Rye to Hastings in Sussex. On the left flank, other landings would take place as far west as Brighton. Minefields on the flanks would protect the forces from approaches by the Royal Navy. But even then, the shipping available was insufficient for the simultaneous massed landings they required. Instead, the forces would have to be brought over in a series of smaller instalments.

Thus the plan for these landings was modified from two echelons to four waves. The first wave would consist of nine divisions, employing about 250 amphibious tanks and 72 rocket-projectors, and accompanied by 38 special ferries fitted up for anti-aircraft protection or bombardment against ground targets. A parachute division would be dropped near Folkestone. The second wave would be made up of four armoured, two motorised and two infantry divisions, with two motorised regiments. Six infantry divisions would make up the third wave. The composition of the fourth wave would be decided upon nearer the date for the invasion. It was expected that a bridgehead 15 miles deep would be created and from this much of Kent and Sussex could be occupied. The armies would then sweep round to the west of London and establish crossings over the Thames.

In addition to the troops involved in these landings, others were assembled in Norway and Holland, instructed to land between Edinburgh and Newcastle, while others in western France were getting ready to occupy southern Ireland. These were, however, deceptions designed to compel the British to spread their defences. Rumours and false reports were spread, apparently practical, to give verisimilitude to these fake landings.

It seems that Hitler believed that Operation Sealion would be successful, provided it could be launched in the autumn of 1940, before the British were able to make good some of the heavy losses in equipment suffered in the Battle of France. Goering, with his propensity for bombastic and ill-considered pronouncements, expressed the view that the Luftwaffe alone could bring Britain to her knees. The army commanders were somewhat cautious about the success of the initial landings but believed that, if the bridgehead was established, Britain would be conquered. They had a high opinion of the fighting qualities of British troops, based partly on their encounters in Belgium, but were less complimentary about British generals. They also believed, with some justification, that the defending forces had insufficient mobility.

Feldwebel Karl Gerdsmeier, a flight engineer, standing in front of his Heinkel He111P-1, G1+AN, of the 5th Staffel, II./Kampfgeschwader 55 at Neu-Ulm, near Ulm in Germany, in April 1940. This aircraft flew in both the Battle of France and the Battle of Britain.

Plans were also drawn up for a system of military government in occupied Britain. Germanic law and order was to be strictly maintained, and various headquarters for police and the Gestapo would be established. Able-bodied men aged between 17 and 45 would be sent to the continent for forced labour. Dissenters would be executed or sent to concentration camps. The country would be stripped of all material available for conducting war. Its stocks of petroleum, much of its foodstuffs and any items of value fancied by the conquerors would be removed. It would become an impoverished and harshly ruled fiefdom of the Third Reich.

On one point, all the German High Commanders were agreed. The key to the invasion's success lay in mastery of the skies. With this achieved, the Luftwaffe could play havoc with the warships of the Royal Navy, strafe and bomb British troops and their defensive positions, paralyse factories and generally spread terror among the civilian population. But the Luftwaffe was not yet ready for a fully fledged attack, for it had also suffered heavy losses in the west. Air historians differ on the extent of these losses, partly because the Luftwaffe-General's returns classified damage to aircraft in terms of percentages, up to 100 per cent for complete loss. Of course aircraft were damaged or destroyed in accidents as well as on operations, with crews injured or killed. Probably the most accurate estimate is 1,700 aircraft destroyed or damaged beyond recovery, although some of the pilots and other aircrews survived to return to their units. The eminent German air historian Dr Horst Boog of the Military History Research Office at Freiburg wrote, 'the Luftwaffe had lost over forty per cent of its aircraft during the campaign in the west and needed time to recover'.

The first German aircraft shot down by British forces in the Second World War was this Dornier Do18D-1 of 2. Staffel, Küstenfliegergruppe 106. It was on patrol over the North Sea on 26 September 1939 when the crew sighted a battle fleet of the Royal Navy. After reporting the position, the flying boat was shot down by a Blackburn Skua from the aircraft carrier HMS *Ark Royal*. The four crew members were rescued by the destroyer HMS *Somali*.

Georges Van Acker collection

The Short Sunderland I, which first entered squadron service in June 1938, had become Coastal Command's premier long-range flying boat by the Battle of Britain. This example, serial L2163, was on the strength of 210 Squadron based at Pembroke Dock before the squadron moved to Oban in Argyll on 13 July 1940. The Sunderland had an impressive war record, being named 'The Flying Porcupine' by the Luftwaffe. On 3 April 1940 a Sunderland of 204 Squadron from Sullom Voe in the Shetlands which was attacked by six Junkers Ju88s over the North Sea shot down one of them, damaged another so badly that it force-landed in Norway, and drove off the remainder.

J. Falconer collection

The Lockheed Hudson I began to enter service with Coastal Command in May 1939. This example, serial P5120, was among the first received in March 1940 by 206 Squadron at Bircham Newton in Norfolk, when they replaced Avro Ansons. Hudsons gave excellent service on reconnaissance and anti-submarine duties from bases around the British Isles as well as from stations abroad. They had a far longer range than the Anson, were better armed and had a greater bomb-carrying capacity. They were less suitable as anti-shipping strike aircraft in daylight, when they came under heavy fire from armed convoys. Later marks of Hudsons were employed on air-sea rescue, on transport work and in meteorological squadrons.

J. Falconer collection

Coastal Command employed Bristol Blenheim IVs as long-distance fighters, fitted with a pack containing four machine-guns under the fuselage, in addition to the normal twin machine-guns in the turret. These Blenheims were on the strength of 254 Squadron, which was equipped with these machines from January 1940 to June 1942.

Author's collection

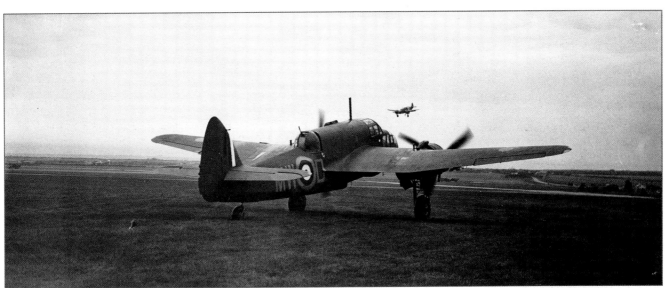

The Bristol Beaufort I, which first entered squadron service in November 1939, was Coastal Command's only torpedo-bomber during the Battle of Britain, when two squadrons operated over the North Sea. Beauforts scored notable successes against enemy ships in northern European waters and in the Mediterranean, but their low-level attacks resulted in a very high loss ratio. The survival rate on an operational tour was rated officially as only 17.5 per cent. This Beaufort I was on the strength of 217 Squadron at St Eval in Cornwall in late 1940. The author joined this squadron in January 1941, as a 19-year-old navigation officer.

J. Falconer collection

A Mark VIII torpedo being loaded on to a Fairey Swordfish of a Fleet Air Arm squadron based at an RAF station.

Author's collection

The Fairey Swordfish I, such as serial L2728 pictured here making a practice drop, was the main torpedo-bomber in service with the Fleet Air Arm during the Battle of Britain. Also used for reconnaissance and mine-laying, it was known affectionately as the 'Stringbag'. Although slow by the standards of the time, it had superb handling characteristics, being capable of landing on a pitching aircraft carrier. Some shore-based Swordfish of the FAA came under the operational control of Coastal Command.

Author's collection

A brand-new Dornier Do17Z-2 before delivery to a Luftwaffe bomber unit. The Do17Z-2 was one of the most successful German bombers and played a prominent part in the Battle of Britain. It had excellent structural strength and could make shallow diving attacks as well as bomb from straight and level flight.

Georges Van Acker collection

This Heinkel He111H-1 coded 1H+EN of II./Kampfgeschwader 26 force-landed on 9 February 1940 near Dalkeith in Midlothian, after combat with a Spitfire 1 of 602 (City of Glasgow) Squadron. It was repaired, given RAF roundels and the serial number AW177, and used for testing purposes.

Philip Jarrett collection

On 16 March 1940 eighteen Junkers Ju88A-1s of 1./Kampfgeschwader 30 from Jever near Wilhelmshaven made shallow dive-bombing attacks on British warships at Scapa Flow in the Orkney Islands, causing minor damage to the cruiser HMS *Norfolk* and the depot ship *Iron Duke*. The crew of this machine, flown by Unteroffizier Werner Mattner, lost their way on the return journey. They made a belly-landing in a meadow near Nakskov Harbour in the Danish island of Lolland in the Baltic Sea and were interned.

Philip Jarrett collection

The Heinkel He60C-1 floatplane was another aircraft employed on air-sea rescue by the Luftwaffe. This example, coded 60+XII, of Jüstenfliegergruppe 106, 1. Seenahauflärungs-Staffel (1.(M)/106), was photographed on the island of Norderney in 1939.

A Messerschmitt Bf109E undergoing
maintenance in the field in early 1940.
J. Falconer collection

These Fairey Battles, powered by a Rolls-Royce Merlin II engine of 1,030hp, were on the strength of the 5th Squadron, 3rd Group, 3rd Aeronautical Regiment of the Belgian Air Force, based at Evere airfield. T-62, T-68 and T-71 from this squadron were sent to bomb the bridge over the Albert Canal at Briegden on 11 May 1940 but were fired upon by Belgian troops. Aircraft T-71 was hit but the slightly wounded crew managed to return to base. The aircraft in the foreground, serial T-63, was probably destroyed when the Luftwaffe bombed the airfield.

Maurice Balasse collection via Jean-Louis Roba

The Belgian Air Force was equipped with eleven Hurricane Is at the outbreak of the Second World War. Armed with four 7.65mm Browning machine-guns, their maximum speed was 318mph. They were not fitted with R/T and had no armour plating. This Hurricane coded H-31 was one of the eleven on the strength of the 2nd Squadron, 2nd Group, 2nd Aeronautical Regiment, known as 'Distel' (Thistle). On 10 May 1940 these Hurricanes were neatly lined up on Schaffen airfield in front of the hangars when they were attacked by Heinkel He111s and nine were destroyed. Ironically, the motto of the Thistle squadron was *Nemo me impune lacessit* (No one touches me with impunity).

Yves Empain collection via Jean-Louis Roba

'ESTUARY ESCORT'
by Charles J. Thompson
Hawker Hurricane I serial N2359 of 17 Squadron, based at Debden in Essex, flying over Thames barges in early May 1940. The squadron was engaged on fighter sweeps over Holland and Belgium during the Blitzkrieg. Detachments were also sent to advanced bases in France.

This Heinkel He111H-4, coded 5J+DM, of Stab II./Kampfgeschader 4, fought an air battle on 18/19 June 1940 with Blenheim IF night-fighters of 23 Squadron based at
Collyweston in Northamptonshire. The crew shot down one Blenheim and damaged another but soon after midnight the Heinkel ditched off Blakeney Harbour in Norfolk.
Major D. *Freiherr* (Count) von Massenbach, the Gruppenkommandeur, was captured with his crew of three.

Philip Jarrett collection

Blenheim IV serial L8856, flown by Pilot Officer
D.S.R. Harriman, was one of three aircraft of
15 Squadron which took off on 15 May 1940
from Wyton in Huntingdonshire to bomb exit
points near Sedan in France where the Germans
had broken through. The starboard propeller fell
off during the return journey and Harriman
made a forced landing at St Kruis in Zeeuws
Vlaanderen, part of the Dutch Province of
Zeeland near the Belgian border. It was not until
after the landing that the crew realised that the
bombs were still on board, for the accumulator
leads had been shot away. The navigator,
Sergeant J.R. Stanford, was injured and taken to
hospital, but Harriman and his gunner managed
to get back to England.

G.J. Zwanenburg collection

CHAPTER THREE

THE DEFENCE
OF BRITAIN

Six weeks of respite from intense operations proved a godsend to the RAF and the other armed services. At the same time, the Government Code and Cypher School was able to improve decryption of enemy signals and acquire a fairly accurate picture of the forces faced by the country. The strengths of the German Army Groups A and B were known, as well as the Order of Battle of the Luftwaffe. It was believed that an attempt at an invasion could come at any time, but there was no knowledge of the probable date or advance information of day-to-day operations.

Increased air attacks by the Luftwaffe might indicate a forthcoming invasion, but meanwhile RAF photo-reconnaissance offered the best chance of guarding against any surprise attack. Fortunately this unit was being improved with new variants of Spitfires and more advanced methods of photo-interpretation. On 8 July 1940 the Photographic Development Unit (PDU) was renamed the Photographic Reconnaissance Unit (PRU). It was then placed under the control of Coastal Command, which was also equipped with twin-engined aircraft partly used for reconnaissance, such as Ansons and Hudsons. The results were passed directly to a Combined Intelligence Committee, which met daily. By July these aircraft were able to bring back photographs of the build-up of German shipping in northern France on a regular basis, providing evidence that any invasion would probably be directed at the beaches of south-east England. They were also able to establish that there was far less sign of such activity in German, Dutch and Belgian ports, or those in north-west and west France. However, there were insufficient long-range aircraft to cover Norway regularly, and at this stage they could not reach the Baltic. Thus the possibility of an expedition from that direction could not be completely dismissed. From time to time there were false alarms from neutral and other sources, and the defence forces were occasionally put on alert.

The Chiefs of Staff were presented with an extraordinary situation when the majority of the British Expeditionary Force returned from France, together with a large number of French soldiers. Almost all the military equipment had been left behind. This included about 485 tanks, over 1,000 heavy guns, 400 anti-tank guns, 90,000 rifles, 8,000 Bren guns, 7,000 tons of ammunition, 38,000 vehicles, 2,000 tractors, 12,000 motor cycles and 8,000 telephones. Thus in early June there existed in Britain the equivalent of twelve army divisions, without mobility or equipment save a few rifles and side-arms.

A low-level oblique photograph of part of the docks at Dunkirk, taken shortly after the British Expeditionary Force had been evacuated. Most of the dock facilities were undamaged at this time.

Author's collection

Winston Churchill, who was not only the Prime Minister but also the Minister of Defence, took the view that improved morale in the fighting services and the civil population could counter-balance the numerical and material advantages possessed by Germany. His stirring and flowing speeches in the House of Commons, also broadcast over the wireless, were astonishingly effective in that respect. On 13 May 1940 he told the British people that he had 'nothing to offer but blood, toil, tears and sweat'. Any politician who said that nowadays would be unlikely to gain points in the opinion polls, but at the time these were exactly the words that most Britons wanted to hear. A famous speech on 4 June 1940 included the moving words: 'We shall fight on the beaches, we shall fight on the landing grounds, we shall fight in the fields and in the streets, we shall fight in the hills; we shall never surrender . . .'. This assurance came as an enormous relief to the people of Britain, although a small political faction led by the Secretary of State for Foreign Affairs, Lord Halifax, believed the military situation was so adverse that the country should negotiate peace with Germany.

The author, who was a very young RAFVR trainee at the time, can verify that the effect of Churchill's speeches was electrifying. The mood of the country changed from a mixture of humiliation, despair and incredulity at the defeat in France to something approaching elation. This defied reason in such a desperate situation, but it would have been a very unwise member of the armed services who openly prophesied the defeat of Britain in that period. Churchill's words also brought a ray of light to those suffering in German-occupied Europe, whose world was otherwise dark and hopeless.

The period after the Battle of France was marked by a great surge of volunteers to join the defence forces in some capacity. For example, the rush to join the Local Defence Volunteers (LDV) was overwhelming. Most of these volunteers were either older men who had served in the First World War, or were in some reserved occupation, or were youngsters who had not reached the age when they could join the army. There were few weapons available at the outset and most were equipped with their own shotguns or improvised pikes until a large consignment of rifles arrived from the USA. Obviously, their military value was limited at this stage, being confined to training, guard duties and observation. In the jocular manner of the times, the LDV was known as 'Look, Duck and Vanish' before being renamed the Home Guard. But there was no doubt of the sincerity of all the recruits and the fighting experience of the older men. As the war progressed, the Home Guard proved its worth by relieving the full-time army of many duties.

In spite of good morale, the full-time army was seriously ill-equipped. The Chief of the Imperial General Staff, General Sir Edmund Ironside, was presented with the unenviable task of making arrangements for defence with inadequate resources. The armaments industry was striving to make good the losses sustained in France, but the delivery of cruiser tanks or armoured vehicles averaged only about 120 a month, wheeled vehicles about 9,000 a month, and field guns about 50 a month. Ironside decided that his troops and their resources should be deployed in depth rather than in a single front line which could be pierced by Blitzkrieg tactics. Some 500 miles of beaches on the south and east

This strange aircraft, Westland Lysander serial K6127, was fitted with twin fins and a mock-up of a four-gun turret. It was tested at the RAF's Aeroplane and Armament Experimental Establishment at Boscombe Down in Wiltshire, and was intended to strafe German troops on the beaches in the event of an invasion.

Author's collection

coasts of England invited enemy landings, and about a third of these were within range of the fighter arm of the Luftwaffe. A combination of static defences along the coasts and inland, plus mobile armoured columns seemed the best solution.

The fixed defences along the coast were reinforced with naval guns and searchlights, while mines were laid out to sea or buried in the beaches. Barbed wire entanglements and other obstructions were built on the beaches. Some roads leading inland were lined with perforated pipes leading to fuel tanks, which could be ignited by the Home Guard from observation posts. Similar pipes were installed on beaches, although efforts to lay them out to sea met with construction difficulties.

Lieutenant-General Sir Alan Brooke, KG, GCB, DSO, on his appointment to the post of Commander-in-Chief of Home Forces on 20 July 1940, when he replaced General Sir Edmund Ironside. Born on 23 July 1883, Field Marshal Lord Alanbrooke died on 17 June 1963.

Bruce Robertson collection

Further inland, another line of anti-tank and other obstacles was erected, taking advantage of natural features such as hills, rivers and canals. This line ran from Richmond in Yorkshire down to the Wash, then via Cambridge to the east of London, and then south of London as far as Bristol, its route based on the assumption that part of the east and south of England had been occupied by the enemy. Mobile divisions were held in reserve, ready to race to any spot where the enemy might achieve a breakthrough. But these were lamentably short of armour. In total, this consisted of less than half that normally supplied to a division, although it was divided among several. On 19 July 1940 Ironside was replaced by General Alan Brooke, who was appointed Commander-in-Chief, Home Forces. Brooke was a younger man who had seen action with the British Expeditionary Force in Belgium and France, and was thus familiar with the new Blitzkrieg tactics.

Britain's other shield against invasion was the Royal Navy, with Admiral of the Fleet Sir Dudley Pound as First Sea Lord. The Home Fleet, commanded by Admiral Sir Charles Forbes, had been weakened by increased responsibilities abroad. Only four battleships were immediately available in June 1940, with two more being refitted. There were also eleven cruisers, an aircraft carrier and eighty destroyers. Many of these commanded the approaches to the North Sea, for the warships of the Kriegsmarine were formidable. The capital ships were stationed outside the range of the Luftwaffe's tactical aircraft, such as the Junkers Ju87s. Only a few of the Royal Navy's warships were at harbours near the beaches where invasions seemed likely. Nineteen destroyers were based at the Humber, Harwich and Sheerness. Five more were at Dover and five at Portsmouth. These were, however, inadequate for the tasks in hand. There were also sloops, corvettes, minesweepers, armed trawlers, harbour defence vessels, gunboats and other small craft.

These warships could not remain static, waiting for a possible invasion. They had onerous duties to perform, such as escorting Atlantic and coastal convoys. When intelligence information was provided, they would move as rapidly as possible to the invasion forces and attempt to wipe out the first waves before they landed. The Royal Navy was as eager as ever to close with the enemy. The men had never forgotten the memorandum issued by Admiral Horatio Nelson on 15 July 1801:

Whatever plans may be adopted, the moment the enemy touch our coast, be it where it may, they are to be attacked by every man afloat and on shore: this must be perfectly understood. Never fear the event.

However, the Admiralty depended largely on RAF reconnaissance, coupled with decryption of enemy signals, to ensure that their warships were in the right places at the right time. Meanwhile retention of an increased number of ships in home waters reduced the escorts available for Atlantic convoys, at a time when the menace of U-boats was growing. More and more merchant ships were being torpedoed and sunk.

The RAF, known as the junior service, became the major player in this desperate time. From early June to mid-July Bomber Command concentrated at night on targets in the Ruhr and northern Germany, with daylight raids by Blenheims against airfields in northern France and the Netherlands. On 3 July the daylight targets included Rhine barges brought into Rotterdam for transport to France and the eventual invasion of Britain. Other aircraft laid magnetic mines outside ports, as did the Beauforts of Coastal Command and the land-based Swordfish of Fleet Air Arm squadrons under its operational control.

By 9 July 1940 Fighter Command consisted of fifty-four operational squadrons in four groups. No. 11 Group in the south-east faced the enemy with thirteen Hurricane, six Spitfire and three Blenheim squadrons. It was commanded by Air Vice-Marshal Keith Park, whose place as Senior Air Staff Officer to Dowding had been taken over by Air Vice-Marshal Douglas Evill. In the eastern counties, No. 12 Group was commanded by Air Vice-Marshal Trafford Leigh-Mallory. This possessed six Hurricane, five Spitfire, one Defiant and two Blenheim squadrons. No. 13 Group in the north of England and Scotland, commanded by Air Vice-Marshal Richard E. Saul, was equipped with six Hurricane, six Spitfire, one Defiant and one Blenheim squadrons. Finally, the newly created No. 10 Group in the south-west of England, commanded by Air Vice-Marshal Sir Quintin Brand, possessed only two Hurricane and two Spitfire squadrons at this stage. These fifty-four squadrons were equipped with about a thousand aircraft, but not all were serviceable at any one time. The six Blenheim squadrons were mainly employed in the night-fighter role. There were also four Hurricane squadrons that were not yet operational.

Dowding's main concerns were the supply of replacement fighters and finding enough pilots to fly them. With the former problem, he had found an unexpected ally. On 17 May 1940, only five days after assuming the posts of Prime Minister and Minister of Defence, Churchill had ordered the Air Ministry to relinquish its control over the Department of Development and Production. Instead, he had created the Ministry of Aircraft Production and appointed his friend Lord Beaverbrook to run it, with a seat on the Cabinet table. Dowding and Beaverbrook were quite dissimilar in character. One was tall, staid, frugal and remote, while the other was tiny, ebullient, wealthy and charismatic. In fact the two men got along famously, possibly because both were patriots, determined to defeat the Luftwaffe, and favoured any method of increasing the production of fighter aircraft, no matter how ruthless or contrary to established procedures.

Beaverbrook also had the support of the Chiefs of Staff, who recognised that the country's immediate salvation depended on its ability to manufacture Spitfires and Hurricanes. He set about his task like a typhoon. Sometimes wheedling and sometimes threatening, he demanded and got from leaders of industry alterations in production lines, at the expense of the new four-engined bombers which were

(Overleaf) A squadron of Hawker Hurricanes on patrol above cloud level.

Author's collection

coming into service. Skilled workers were diverted to the more essential parts of the industry, more women were recruited and sub-contractors were appointed. Factory throughput times were telescoped, partly by diverting production from the manufacture of spare parts, which hitherto had taken up over 15 per cent of total output, to the manufacture of complete aircraft.

Even before Beaverbrook took up his new position, the output of new and repaired fighters had been rising steadily. In May 1940, 325 were produced, compared with 261 planned, and 446 were produced in the following month, against 292 planned. The losses in France were made good and all the fighter squadrons were back to full strength, some with an extra reserve of aircraft. It is difficult to assess whether Beaverbrook's measures were entirely responsible for this rapid increase in production. Perhaps his main achievement was in the repairs organisation. Many fighters that had been damaged in combat or in flying accidents were awaiting spare parts which were a long time in arriving. He demanded that these aircraft be 'cannibalised', creating serviceable machines from parts obtained from other damaged aircraft. During the Battle of Britain repaired fighters accounted for nearly 40 per cent of those reaching the operational squadrons. However, his disruption of factory flows certainly resulted in a decline in the overall output of aircraft for the RAF. This became manifest in the figures for the final quarter of 1940 and the first quarter of 1941, before they picked up again.

Dowding's other worry was the supply of skilled fighter pilots, and this was more difficult to satisfy. Some of the best men had been lost in the Battle of France, and most of those who had not been killed were prisoners of war. About 1,050 pilots remained to man his fifty-four squadrons and the four which were still non-operational, but more squadrons were likely to be formed in the next few weeks. Appeals for more pilots resulted in about fifty volunteers from the Fleet Air Arm. It was possible that in the expected air actions, some of these RAF and FAA pilots would bale out over land or crash-land their machines. If uninjured, they would be able to return to their squadrons. Otherwise Dowding would have to rely on newcomers from the training units, eager but inexperienced, mostly those who had begun their training before the war.

There were too few training schools to meet the influx of wartime entrants, as the author was to discover after volunteering on 3 September 1939. Once attested as a trainee pilot or navigator, these volunteers were sent home on indefinite leave to await a place in the Initial Training Wings. After about three months they were called to begin a course of ground instruction which should have lasted about two months but was steadily extended. Even after this, most trainees were dispersed to various airfields as ground gunners, having learnt something about machine-guns without firing them. It was an extremely frustrating time. Eventually, places became available in the Flying Training Schools in Britain. Unfavourable weather then caused delays, and there were too few qualified instructors. The system did not begin to produce a steady and adequate supply of pilots and navigators until places for trainee pilots were offered in America and the Empire Air Training Scheme came on stream.

Another defect in the arrangements for defence was the absence of a comprehensive air-sea rescue system. The pilots were issued with Mae West lifejackets, of the early type with a tube and a screw-top nozzle which one blew through to inflate after landing in the sea. But the K-type pilot's dinghy which was carried as a seat pack later in the war did not exist in 1940. Nor was there a comprehensive organisation for picking up ditched pilots, who might be injured, suffering from shock or dying from hypothermia. An experimental air-sea rescue

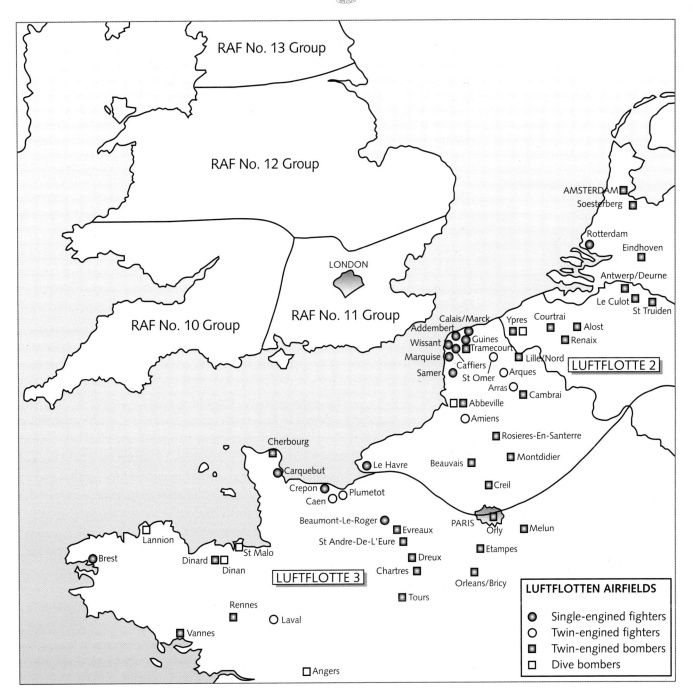

Luftflotten 2 and 3 in July 1940.

launch had been developed for Coastal Command before the war and several of these were on order, but at the beginning of the Battle of Britain there were no systematic arrangements for carrying out searches by sea or air. It was a matter of luck, with the pilot hoping that one of his comrades had seen him and that a lifeboat would be called out. Other than that, he had to hope that he would be spotted by the coastguard services or the crew of a fishing vessel.

At the same time that Fighter Command was making its preparations, the Luftwaffe gathered its strength for the forthcoming battle. The chain of command ran from Hitler to Reichsmarschall Hermann Goering with his deputy and Inspector-General of the Luftwaffe, Generalfeldmarschall Erhard Milch, to the heads of three Luftflotten assigned the task of paving the way for an invasion of Britain. These heads had been promoted after the victories in Scandinavia and the west. Luftflotte 2, commanded by Generalfeldmarschall Albert Kesselring,

YOUR FOOD IN
WAR-TIME

PUBLIC INFORMATION
LEAFLET　　NO. 4

Read this and
keep it carefully.
You may need it.

Issued from the Lord Privy Seal's Office July, 1939

J. Falconer collection

was responsible for the assault from bases in the Low Countries and north-east France. Luftflotte 3, under Generalfeldmarschall Hugo Sperrle, was based in the north and west of France. The total strength of these two air fleets amounted to about 1,200 long-range bombers, 400 dive-bombers and 1,100 fighters. Of these, the fighters and dive-bombers were based at forward airfields near the coasts, with the long-range bombers further inland. Most faced Air Vice-Marshal Park's No. 11 Group in south-east England, with about 350 serviceable aircraft, and Air Vice-Marshal Sir Quintin Brand's No. 10 Group, with about fifty serviceable aircraft. Luftflotte 5, commanded by Generalfeldmarschall Hans-Juergen Stumpff, was a much smaller air fleet based in Denmark and Norway, intended primarily for diversionary operations over the north-east of England. It ensured that Fighter Command kept several squadrons away from the south-east.

The orders of these Luftflotten were to blockade the British Isles by attacks on ports or shipping, coupled with the mining of sea lanes and harbour entrances, and to achieve complete air supremacy over the RAF as a preliminary to Operation Sealion, the invasion of southern England. Above all, they were required to bring Fighter Command to battle and wipe it out.

The German pilots and other aircrews were full of confidence. The Luftwaffe had shared in victories won at lightning speed in Poland, Scandinavia and the west. Although it had suffered quite severe losses, some of the airmen taken prisoner had been able to return to their units. The aircrews had acquired a respect for the RAF but believed that their equipment and tactics were superior. The Messerschmitt Bf109E – the 'Emil' – was considered far better than either the Hurricane or the Spitfire, and indeed it was somewhat faster and had a higher rate of climb. The Messerschmitt Bf110 twin-engined 'Destroyer' was highly regarded and crewed by the cream of the Luftwaffe. The Junkers Ju87 Stuka dive-bomber had enjoyed a fearsome reputation as the spearhead of the Blitzkrieg, with its steep dive, screamer switched on, and a high degree of bombing accuracy. The Heinkel He111, Junkers Ju88 and Dornier Do17 long-range bombers were soundly built, could absorb much punishment, and were crewed by experienced men. Some of these bombers utilised a radio navigational aid named *Knickebein* (crooked leg), which sent out a series of dashes on the port side and dots on the starboard side. These merged into a single narrow beam when the aircraft was dead on track. When this crossed another beam, it gave the bomb aimer a fairly accurate position for dropping the bombs on a chosen target. The aid had an effective range of about 250 miles when the bomber flew at about 15,000ft, but much less at low altitudes. The bombing force also possessed a pathfinder unit, Kampfgruppe 100.

But some of these advantages were illusory, as events in the next few weeks would demonstrate. The Bf109 was a first-class machine in the hands of an experienced pilot but it was not easy to fly and suffered from a high rate of accidents, even when taxying. Its radius of action was little better than 200 miles and far less when using fuel while forming up with bombers and then becoming involved in combat; this meant that fighters based in France could seldom penetrate north of the Thames. The radius of action of the Junkers Ju87 was even less, at about 175 miles, unless it carried drop-tanks. Its bomb-load was normally about 1,000lb. The maximum speed was about 230mph, and with limited armament it was very vulnerable to Hurricanes and Spitfires, especially when pulling out of a dive. The Messerschmitt Bf110 was fast and had a much greater radius of action at 340 miles without extra tanks. It was very useful for reconnaissance and surprise attacks but its lack of manoeuvrability and sluggish acceleration made it a fairly easy target for single-engined fighters.

(*Opposite*) 'THE ROCHFORD BOYS'
by Charles J. Thompson
Spitfire Is of 54 Squadron from Rochford in Essex, a satellite of RAF Hornchurch, roaring over Westcliff-on-Sea during the Battle of Britain. The artist used his son and daughter-in-law as adult models, outside their house, to portray the children in the painting. The car parked in the road is a wartime Morris 10. In the left foreground, railings have been removed to provide iron for war production.

The longer-range bombers had an ample radius of action. The He111 could carry up to 4,400lb of bombs, the Ju88 about 4,000lb, but the Do17 only about 2,200lb. However, all three were vulnerable to single-engined fighters. They were armed with single 7.92mm machine-guns in various positions, but an air gunner firing one of these against a fighter armed with eight machine-guns usually came off worse in the encounter. Even in formation, the bombers could be picked off by fighters. A malfunctioning or damaged engine meant dropping behind, and the fighters would then take turns in knocking the aircraft out of the sky. The bombers were largely dependent on the Messerschmitt Bf109s to keep the enemy away from them. Quite apart from the danger from Hurricanes and Spitfires in daylight operations, they also had to face anti-aircraft fire, or avoid balloons if they came down below about 7,000ft.

The major defect of the Luftwaffe in the Battle of Britain was that it was primarily a tactical air force, employed in combination with armies. It had been highly successful in that role, but when employed as a strategic air force on daylight operations, single-engined fighters fitted with long-range tanks were required to escort the bombers. In any event there were insufficient single-engined fighters of any variant for a sustained campaign. German aircraft production had concentrated on the bombers favoured by Hitler for his aggressive Luftflotten. The output of the Bf109 was only about 125 a month in early 1940 and seldom exceeded 375 a month at the height of the Battle of Britain. The corresponding figure for output plus repairs of Hurricanes and Spitfires was over 500 a month at the beginning of the battle, increasing to about 600 thereafter.

German Intelligence was partly accurate and partly defective. There had been plenty of opportunity to interrogate British and French prisoners, either by direct means or surreptitiously by hidden microphones in cells shared by two men. The Germans knew that Fighter Command stood at about fifty operational squadrons and that it possessed about twenty aircraft per squadron. Their estimate of 60 per cent Hurricanes to 40 per cent Spitfires was reasonably accurate. They assumed, incorrectly, that there were plenty of well-trained pilots. They knew that there were numerous airfields with satellite airstrips in south-east England but were sceptical about the adequacy of the maintenance and supply arrangements. Their estimate of fighter production was seriously inaccurate at between 180 to 300 a month, probably because the prisoners had no idea of the numbers. They formed the impression that a few weeks of air operations would be sufficient to wipe out the defending fighters and enable the invasion to begin.

Perhaps their worst error was to believe that the command structure was outdated and inflexible. This probably stemmed from the ingrained belief in Germany, originating from a conversation between General Erich Ludendorff and General Max Hoffman in the First World War and apparently confirmed by their victories in Belgium and France during the Blitzkrieg, that the British military consisted of 'lions led by donkeys'. They knew that the RAF had RDF coverage but had no idea that it had been organised so efficiently, or that it had largely eliminated the need for standing patrols and could scramble Hurricanes and Spitfires so effectively.

In spite of these strengths and weaknesses on both sides, no impartial observer with full knowledge of the facts could have forecast the outcome of the battle with any confidence. So much depended on the skill and resolution of the pilots and aircrews involved, and the organisations which backed them. All that could have been known was that the future of the western world would depend on the RAF's victory – or its defeat.

Many pillboxes were hastily erected with reinforced concrete as strongpoints against the invasion. This one was manned by soldiers armed with Bren guns, rifles and grenades.

Author's collection

Army motor-cyclists on patrol along the Sussex Downs.

Author's collection

Men of the Green Howards, a regiment which had fought in the Battle of France, under training on the south coast of England. They are rushing to take up defensive positions against a mock invasion.

Author's collection

The Green Howards in defensive positions among the coarse grass, aiming at a beach where the enemy might land.

Author's collection

Troops of the Northern Command under training, with live machine-gun bullets making a furrow and kicking up the sand in front of their heads.

Author's collection

A sniper concealed in the hollow trunk of a fallen tree, during an anti-invasion exercise.

Author's collection

Infantry of the Northern Command under training, crossing a stream under a barrage of heavy shells.

Author's collection

An A13 Cruiser tank named 'Condor' during an
anti-invasion exercise in the Eastern Counties.
Author's collection

A Bofors light anti-aircraft gun in action against
low-flying enemy aircraft at night.

Author's collection

Britain's defences around the coasts included
9.2in howitzers, each firing a shell weighing
350lb. This howitzer has fired in practice and the
barrel is in full recoil, while the discharge has
formed a smoke ring.

Author's collection

A flight mechanic of the WAAF working on an engine while under training.

Author's collection

'Messerschmitt chases a British Spitfire' was the title of this photograph when it was published in the German magazine *Der Adler* in the summer of 1940. This was a mock combat. Spitfire IB serial P9331 of the RAF's Photographic Development Unit was captured intact by the Wehrmacht in France and used for experimental purposes, as shown here with a Messerschmitt Bf109E. The Spitfire carried the letters G and Y. It was also photographed in mock combat with a Heinkel He111 and a Dornier Do17Z in 1940, followed by an encounter with a Focke-Wulf Fw190 in late 1941.

Georges Van Acker collection

Belgian soldiers who escaped during the battles for their country and France were re-equipped and retrained in England to form a new fighting force. Five Belgian motor-cyclists demonstrate their method of crossing a stream without getting their feet wet.

Author's collection

WAR EMERGENCY

INFORMATION AND INSTRUCTIONS

Read this leaflet carefully and make sure that you and all other responsible persons in your house understand its contents.

Pay no attention to rumours. Official news will be given in the papers and over the wireless.

Listen carefully to all broadcast instructions and be ready to note them down.

Issued by the Ministry of Information on behalf o the War Office and the Ministry of Home Security

STAY WHERE YOU ARE

IF this island is invaded by sea or air everyone who is not under orders must stay where he or she is. This is not simply advice : it is an order from the Government, and you must obey it just as soldiers obey their orders. Your order is " Stay Put ", but remember that **this does not apply until invasion comes.**

Why must I stay put?

Because in France, Holland and Belgium, the Germans were helped by the people who took flight before them. Great crowds of refugees blocked all roads. The soldiers who could have defended them could not get at the enemy. The enemy used the refugees as a human shield. These refugees were got out on to the roads by rumour and false orders. Do not be caught out in this way. Do not take any notice of any story telling what the enemy has done or where he is. Do not take orders except from the Military, the Police, the Home Guard (L.D.V.) and the A.R.P. authorities or wardens.

What will happen to me if I don't stay put?

If you do not stay put you will stand a very good chance of being killed. The enemy may machine-gun you from the air in order to increase panic, or you may run into enemy forces which have landed behind you. An official German message was captured in Belgium which ran :

" Watch for civilian refugees on the roads. Harass them as much as possible."

Our soldiers will be hurrying to drive back the invader and will not be able to stop and help you. On the contrary, they will have to turn *you* off the roads so that they can get at the enemy. You will not have reached safety and you will have done just what the enemy wanted you to do.

How shall I prepare to stay put?

Make ready your air-raid shelter; if you have no shelter prepare one. Advice can be obtained from your local Air Raid Warden or in " Your Home as an Air-raid Shelter ", the Government booklet which tells you how to prepare a shelter in your house that will be strong enough to protect you against stray shots and falling metal. If you can have a trench ready in your garden or field, so much the better, especially if you live where there is likely to be danger from shell-fire.

How can I help?

You can help by setting a good example to others. Civilians who try to join in the fight are more likely to get in the way than to help. The defeat of an enemy attack is the task of the armed forces which include the Home Guard, so if you wish to fight enrol in the Home Guard. If there is no vacancy for you at the moment register your name for enrolment and you will be called upon as soon as the Army is ready to employ you. For those who cannot join there are many ways in which the Military and Home Guard may need your help in their preparations. Find out what you can do to help in any local defence work that is going on, and be ready to turn your hand to anything if asked by the Military or Home Guard to do so.

If you are responsible for the safety of a factory or some other important building, get in touch with the nearest military authority. You will then be told how your defence should fit in with the military organisation and plans.

What shall I do if the Invader comes my way?

If fighting by organised forces is going on in your district and you have no special duties elsewhere, go to your shelter and stay there till the battle is past. Do not attempt to join in the fight. Behave as if an air-raid were going on. The enemy will seldom turn aside to attack separate houses.

But if small parties are going about threatening persons and property in an area not under enemy control and come your way, you have the right of every man and woman to do what you can to protect yourself, your family and your home.

Stay put.

It's easy to say. When the time comes it may be hard to do. But you have got to do it; and in doing it you will be fighting Britain's battle as bravely as a soldier.

(Printed in England)

J. Falconer collection

The Women's Land Army was re-formed in June 1939, having been disbanded after the First World War. The Ministry of Agriculture requested an experiment to check whether volunteer girls could replace men in the heavy work of threshing corn. A course lasting three weeks took place at Coldblow Farm at Detling in Kent, with satisfactory results.

Author's collection

Volunteers in the Women's Land Army collecting hay at the Essex Institute of Agriculture, where they were trained in all kinds of farm and dairy work. The 'Suffolk Punch' horse was widespread in East Anglia at the time. It was small but sturdy, chestnut in colour and admirable as a draught horse.

Author's collection

A Cornish farmer saves time by having his crop of broccoli packed on a road, ready to be collected by a lorry, instead of on his fields.

Author's collection

French troops evacuated from Dunkirk practising mortar fire in England. They are still wearing their original uniforms and helmets but are equipped with British gas-masks.

Author's collection

The Thames estuary provided a gap in London's balloon defences through which German bombers could fly. Thus a string of barges was moored between Southend-on-Sea on the north bank and Sheerness on the south bank, a distance of 7 miles. Each barge was skippered by a civilian but the crew included RAF men responsible for a standard balloon, as shown in this photograph. East of this line, more balloons were flown from drifters, which were normally used for drift-net fishing and were better able to weather the rough seas. The RAF men came under the authority of 952 (Thames Barrage) Squadron.

Bruce Robertson collection

Merchant convoys around the coasts of Britain were protected by the RAF's Mobile Balloon Barrage Flotilla. The censor has removed what appears to be a very large warship, probably a cruiser, in the background of this photograph.

Author's collection

Home Guard officers under training with a Lysander, learning how to aim, direct and control rifle fire at an enemy aircraft such as the Junkers Ju87 Stuka dive-bomber.

Author's collection

Men of the Local Defence Volunteers under training. This part-time force was formed on 14 May 1940, during the Battle of France, and by the end of that month about 300,000 men had volunteered. There were insufficient uniforms but the men were issued with LDV armbands. Almost no arms were available but about a million Enfield P-14 rifles of .300in calibre, left over from the First World War and packed in grease, were purchased from the USA. Four of these rifles are shown here. The LDV was renamed the Home Guard on 31 July 1940.

Author's collection

Tactical instruction being given to members of the Home Guard at a War Office Training School. The lecturer is illustrating a grenade.

Author's collection

Men of the Home Guard practising with a Lewis gun in the highlands of Scotland, overlooking a loch. A large proportion of the volunteers in this area were stalkers and gamekeepers who knew every inch of the remote countryside.

Author's collection

Men of the Home Guard, kitted out with khaki uniforms, rifles and gas masks, practising aiming at a moving saloon car as an alternative to a low-flying aircraft.

Author's collection

Coastal defences of Eastern Command keeping watch at night in late July 1940, in preparation for the expected German invasion.

Author's collection

CHAPTER FOUR

OPENING ROUNDS

The first task for the Luftwaffe was to establish air superiority over part of the English Channel and to deny its use to the Royal Navy as well as to Fighter Command. The commanders intended to engage the Hurricanes and Spitfires in a battle of attrition they were sure they would win. This part of the Channel was also the area in which the German seaborne invasion was planned to take place. In addition to these daylight operations, the Luftwaffe continued to make a number of small harassing attacks at night on ports and industrial centres.

The coastal traffic in these waters was principally concerned with the transport of food and coal to places within Britain, thus relieving pressure on the overburdened railway system. None of the Atlantic convoys passed through these waters, since in early July they had been diverted to the approaches north of Ireland, increasing their distance from German bombers based in France. Shipping bound for the east coast passed round the north of Scotland. However, all shipping round the British coasts required some fighter protection, putting an extra strain on Dowding's limited resources.

An air division, known as a Fliegerkorps, from each Luftflotten was assigned to this first phase in the Channel. In the Pas de Calais II. Fliegerkorps under General Bruno Lörzer, part of Luftflotte 2, was given the task of clearing the Straits of Dover. From the area of Le Havre VIII. Fliegerkorps under Generalmajor Wolfram Freiherr von Richthofen, part of Luftflotte 3, operated to the Isle of Wight. Von Richthofen, a cousin of the famous pilot Manfred Freiherr von Richthofen, was a specialist in dive-bomber tactics.

The German commanders were confident that their task could be completed without great difficulty and assigned only part of their forces to the operation in two Battle Groups. The one in the east consisted of about 75 Dornier Do17s, about 60 Junkers Ju87 Stukas and some 200 Messerschmitt Bf109 escorts. Its bomber force was commanded by Oberst Johannes Fink, who was appointed Kanalkampfführer (Channel Battle Leader). Although 50 years old, he continued to fly on bomber missions. There were two Jagdgeschwaders (Fighter Groups), JG51 commanded by Oberst Theo Osterkamp, a First World War ace who had been credited with thirty-two kills and who also continued to fly operationally, and JG26 commanded by Major Adolf Galland. The ace pilot with the highest score of victories in the Battle of Britain was Major Werner Mölders in JG51.

Generalleutnant (Lieutenant-General) Adolf 'Dolfo' Galland was born on 19 March 1912 in Westerholt, Westphalia, and became one of Germany's most celebrated fighter aces. He fought in the Condor Legion in Spain, against Poland and in the Battle of France. He was appointed Gruppenkommandeur (Group Commander) of III./Jagdgeschwader 26 'Schlageter' in June 1940, during the Battle of Britain, and promoted to Major the following month. On 21 August 1940 he was appointed Geschwaderkommodore (Wing Commander) of Jagdgeschwader 26 by Goering. His awards were the Knight's Cross on 29 July 1940, followed by the Swords on 24 September 1940. On 1 November 1940 he became an Oberst and a year later 'General of the Fighter Arm'. When credited with ninety-four victories, he was invested on 28 January 1942 with the Knight's Cross with Oak Leaves, Swords and Diamonds. Promotion to Generalmajor followed on 19 November 1942 and then Generalleutnant on 1 November 1944. Although he fell out of favour with Goering, he commanded Jagdverband (Fighter formation) 44 in January 1945, equipped with Messerschmitt M262 jet aircraft and attacking Allied bomber formations, thereby increasing his victories to 104. He became an aviation consultant after the war and was a welcome speaker at RAF reunions. He died on 9 February 1996 at the age of 84.

Bruce Robertson collection

The Battle Group in the west consisted of Messerschmitt Bf109 and Bf110 fighters with about 250 Junkers Ju87 dive-bombers. This group was assigned the task of clearing shipping from the area around Portsmouth.

The campaign began on 3 July, although not in any great strength, with formations seeking convoys or isolated shipping. Luftflotte 3 in the west scored a success on the following day when Junkers Ju88s bombed and sank the auxiliary anti-aircraft (AAA) ship HMS *Foylebank* of 5,500 tons in Portland Harbour. Another success followed on 9 July when the sloop HMS *Foxglove* of 1,165 tons was badly damaged south of Nab Tower on the Isle of Wight and towed into Portsmouth Dockyard. It was on this day that the fighter ace Flight Lieutenant A.C. 'Al' Deere, a New Zealander in the RAF, had a narrow escape. A flight commander with 54 Squadron, equipped with Spitfires and based at Rochford in Essex, Deere was leading a formation on his fourth flight of the day when he came across a German rescue floatplane escorted by several Messerschmitt Bf109s. A dogfight ensued and Deere fired at one Bf109 and then tackled another. They approached head-on, both firing, and the Spitfire was hit. Then the two aircraft collided, the Bf109 scraping along the top of the Spitfire. With his propeller badly bent and the engine switched off, Deere managed to glide his machine to Kent and crash-land in a field near RAF Manston. The canopy jammed but he wrenched it open while ammunition exploded in the flames. He struggled clear, bruised but otherwise unhurt. It was not known what happened to the Bf109.

It soon became evident to Fighter Command that the defending aircraft were sometimes unable to reach high altitudes quickly enough to intercept the German formations after these had been picked up by the RDF stations. Some flights from the squadrons were moved to forward airfields nearer the coast. On average twelve coastal convoys required protection during each day, placing a considerable burden on No. 11 Group. Dowding had not catered for this eventuality and he limited his commitment in order to avoid depletion of his force before the expected assault over the mainland.

Nevertheless, aircraft on both sides were shot down, while the conflicts enabled Fighter Command's headquarters at Bentley Priory to gain experience

Werner Mölders, one of Germany's ace fighter pilots, was born on 18 March 1913 in Geilenkirchen. After joining the Luftwaffe he flew from March 1937 to mid-1938 as a Staffelkapitän in the Condor Legion in Spain, scoring many victories. His first success against the RAF was on 30 October 1939 when he shot down a Bristol Blenheim. By 27 May 1940 he had been credited with twenty victories and became the first fighter pilot to receive the Knight's Cross. However, on 5 June he was shot down by a Dewoitine 520 of the French Air Force and became a prisoner until after the Armistice. He then served in Jagdgeschwader 51 of Luftflotte 2 against Britain and was made Kommodore on 27 July 1940. By 15 July 1941 he had been credited with 101 victories. He was killed on 22 November 1941 when flying in a Heinkel He111 during bad weather.

Georges Van Acker collection

HEFT 21 / BERLIN, 15. OKTOBER 1940

Denmark	35 Öre	Finland	3.50 Fmk.
Holland	15 cents	Norway	35 Öre
Sweden	45 Öre	U.S.A.	8 Cents

HERAUSGEGEBEN UNTER MITWIRKUNG DES REICHS-LUFTFAHRTMINISTERIUMS

Major Werner Mölders

Kommodore eines Jagdgeschwaders, dem der Führer als erstem der erfolgreichen Jagdflieger nach dem 40. Luftsieg das Eichenlaub zum Ritterkreuz des Eisernen Kreuzes verlieh

Major (Squadron Leader) Werner Mölders, Commodore of a fighter wing, the first of the German aces to be decorated by the Führer with the Oak Leaves to the Knight's Cross of the Iron Cross

The German magazine *Der Adler* by August Scherl Verlag began publication shortly before the outbreak of the Second World War, in collaboration with the Reichsluftfahrtministerium (German Air Ministry). It concentrated on the successes of the Luftwaffe. The German edition was also sold in Bulgaria, Croatia, Denmark, Finland, Greece, Hungary, the Netherlands, Norway, Sweden and Switzerland. Another edition was printed in French and sold in Belgium, France, Portugal, Romania and Switzerland. A German–English edition was sold in the United States up to mid-1941. The final edition was published in early 1945.

Georges Van Acker collection

A group of high-ranking Luftwaffe officers. Left to right: General der Flieger Hans Jeschonnek, Chief of Staff; Generalfeldmarschall Albert Kesselring; Oberst Wilhelm Speidel, Chief of Staff of Luftflotte 2; General der Flieger Bruno Lörzer, commander of II. Fliegerkorps. Kesselring was born on 30 November 1885 in Bavaria. On 20 July 1904 he enlisted in the 2nd Bavarian Foot Artillery Regiment and became a Fahnenjunker (Colour Sergeant). Later in the First World War he was recommended for an appointment to the General Staff. He remained in the army after the war but transferred to the new Luftwaffe in October 1933, becoming head of the Administration Office and then rising to other posts. General der Flieger Kesselring was head of Luftflotte 1 in Poland at the outbreak of the Second World War but in early 1940 moved to take over Luftflotte 2 in the west. On 19 July 1940 Hitler appointed him Generalfeldmarschall of the Luftwaffe. He remained in the west until 21 December 1941 when he became Commander-in-Chief of the Armed Forces South (Italy and North Africa). He relinquished command of Luftflotte 2 in 1943 and remained in command of the German forces in Italy until 10 March 1945. From 25 March until 6 May 1945 he was responsible for combat operations in western Germany. He died in Bad Nauheim on 16 July 1960.

Author's collection

and proficiency in its control system. It was also realised that self-sealing tanks for fighters were required, for horrible injuries were caused to pilots trapped in flames. The RAF had been slow in providing these. Another requirement was the constant-speed propeller, but these were now being fitted to the fighters. It was also in this period that some of the German pilots began to appreciate that the British RDF system was remarkably effective, with fighters being vectored on to them as soon as they neared their targets. However, their reports were not given much credence by the German High Commanders, who continued to believe that the RAF fighters were controlled solely from their stations and lacked flexibility.

German fighter tactics in the Battle of France had been shown to be superior to those of the RAF. A Staffel (squadron) of twelve aircraft was deployed in three Schwarme (flights) of four aircraft apiece, which in turn were broken down into two Rotte (sections) of two aircraft. This loose formation gave the German fighters far more flexibility than the RAF method, which had been to employ a squadron of twelve in four tight vics of three, formating so closely on each other that the pilots spent most of their time looking at their leader instead of keeping watch for enemy aircraft.

In this new situation, with enemy fighters within range of the south of England, Fighter Command instructed its squadrons to patrol higher than the enemy and concentrate on shooting down the bombers. An upper squadron would draw off the fighter escorts, which were regarded primarily as decoys. These instructions were set out in Memorandum no. 8 of 3 June, which invited comments from the Group Commanders. Air Vice-Marshal Saul of No. 13 Group replied by recommending that each squadron of twelve aircraft be deployed in three flights of four, with each flight split into pairs, on the lines of the German method. Air Vice-Marshal Park of No. 11 Group recommended that each squadron of twelve aircraft should be divided into six sections of two apiece, arranged in line astern, with the wingman protecting the leader. Air Vice-Marshal Leigh-Mallory did not reply until 25 July, when he enclosed from one of his squadron commanders a recommendation of the use of pairs in combat, and from another a report opposing the use of 'Big Wings'. The latter was in contrast to Leigh-Mallory's own advocacy of Big Wings a few weeks later. Meanwhile, the various squadron commanders in all Groups seem to have adopted whatever formations they considered advisable.

At a later stage Dowding chose 10 July as the historic date for the commencement of the Battle of Britain, although many combats had taken place beforehand. Certainly there was a fairly major assault on this day, when a convoy near Dover was attacked by about twenty Dornier Do17s escorted by numerous Bf110s and Bf109s. Hurricanes patrolling over the convoy went into the attack and were joined by sections from other squadrons. Other German bombers attacked Swansea and Falmouth. On this day, some of the Bf110s went into a circle in an attempt to protect one another from the single-engined fighters, demonstrating that the crews knew they were vulnerable. The two Luftflotten lost twenty-five aircraft destroyed or badly damaged on that day, including five Bf110s. The RAF lost twelve aircraft, but ten pilots were unhurt in crash-landings and their damaged aircraft were repairable.

The pace continued during the next day, with VIII. Fliegerkorps despatching Junkers Ju87s and Messerschmitt BF109s in the early morning to attack a convoy sailing off the coast of Dorset. These were tackled by Spitfires and Hurricanes, with losses on both sides. The Fliegerkorps tried again in the afternoon, with Messerschmitt Bf110s escorting the Stukas, and again an air battle ensued. A third attack was made with Heinkel He111s escorted by Bf110s.

The day was costly for the attackers, for seventeen aircraft failed to return and eight came back severely damaged. One of the latter was a Dornier Do17Z of 4./Kampfgeschwader 2 which landed at Arras with three of its four crew members wounded. It had been in combat near Southwold in Suffolk with a Hurricane of 85 Squadron flown from Martlesham Heath by the commanding officer, Squadron Leader Peter W. Townsend. The German aircraft was badly hit but kept on flying. One of its bullets hit the coolant system of the Hurricane and the engine stopped. Townsend was forced to bale out but was lucky enough to be picked up by the trawler *Cap Finisterre* and brought into Harwich. Another German aircraft was shot down by a Hurricane of 242 (Canadian) Squadron flown from North Weald in Essex by the commanding officer, the remarkable Squadron Leader Douglas Bader. This was a Dornier Do17 of Wetterer-kundungsstaffel 26, a weather reconnaissance unit. The four members of the crew were killed. Fighter Command lost five aircraft on this day, with three pilots killed, as well as six other aircraft damaged.

Between 13 and 18 July there were more shipping attacks off Dover and the Dorset coast, but unfavourable weather restricted some activities. The Germans lost twenty-three aircraft in combat or accidentally in these five days, with thirty-five others severely damaged by the RAF or in domestic accidents. Fighter Command lost ten fighters in combat, with six others destroyed accidentally and twenty-eight damaged but repairable.

The next day, 19 July, is notable for the eclipse of the Defiant two-seater as a front-line day-fighter. These aircraft had achieved some initial success in the Battle of France when 264 Squadron, based at Duxford, operated in conjunction with Hurricanes. The single-seater fighters attacked the Luftwaffe formations from behind while the Defiants made cross-over attacks from underneath, firing upwards into the exposed bellies of enemy aircraft. The crews claimed as many as sixty-five aircraft destroyed in such encounters, until the German pilots began to understand the unusual tactics. Fourteen Defiants were shot down in this

(*Overleaf*) On 11 July 1940 Heinkel He111H G1+LK of 2./Kampfgeschwader 55 was shot down by two Hurricane Is of 145 Squadron based at Tangmere in Sussex, while on a sortie against Portsmouth dockyard. It force-landed near Selsey Bill and burst into flames. Two of the crew were killed and three were wounded and captured.

Philip Jarrett collection

period, although some of the crews managed to reach Allied lines and return to England, their morale still high.

On 13 July another Defiant squadron, no. 141, was moved down from Turnhouse near Edinburgh to West Malling in Kent. Six days later, on 19 July, nine of these two-seater fighters were sent up on patrol without supporting Hurricanes or Spitfires. They were at about 5,000ft off Dover when fifteen Messerschmitt Bf109s of III./Jagdgeschwader 51 dived out of the sun, led by Hauptmann Hannes Trautloft. Five Defiants were shot down almost immediately and crashed into the sea or on land, killing all crew members save one who was wounded but rescued from the sea. Two other Defiants were damaged and in both cases the gunners baled out, with one survivor. The two pilots crash-landed and survived. Doubtless the formation would have been completely wiped out if Hurricanes of 111 Squadron had not come to its rescue.

On this day of disaster for the Defiants, six other aircraft in Fighter Command were damaged in combat but repairable. The Germans lost six aircraft and ten damaged, thus gaining a short ascendancy over the RAF. The remainder of 141 Squadron was sent up to RAF Prestwick two days later, where the Defiants carried out good work in the night-fighter role in the defence of Glasgow. On the same day 264 Squadron was withdrawn to Kirton-on-Lindsey in Lincolnshire, in a similar role.

Only one flight of Gladiator IIs remained in the RAF in this period, based at Sumburgh in the Shetlands, from where the biplanes were engaged on patrols over the North Sea with little result apart from a couple of inconclusive engagements with Heinkel He111s. This flight was sent down to Roborough in Devon on 21 July, having been replaced by a flight of Hurricanes detached from 232 Squadron at Wick in Caithness. The Gladiators were engaged on defensive patrols, mainly at night, in an attempt to guard against bombing attacks on the great naval base at Plymouth. Their numbers were augmented and the flight was enlarged until it became 247 Squadron on 1 August. There was little activity and replacement Hurricanes did not arrive until the following November, after the end of the Battle of Britain.

On 20 July shipping off Dover was attacked once more, by Stukas escorted by Bf109s. The destroyer HMS *Brazen* was damaged and later sank in tow. During this and other air battles in the area the attackers lost twelve aircraft and six damaged. Fighter Command lost eight aircraft with four damaged but repairable. There was far less activity on the following day, but the Germans lost twelve aircraft plus six damaged for various reasons while Fighter Command had one aircraft destroyed in an accident and five others damaged but repairable. On 23 July there were few encounters in poor weather but the Luftwaffe lost five aircraft and four damaged for various reasons, while Fighter Command lost two accidentally and six damaged. Two of the latter were in combat but all six were repairable.

Raids against shipping were resumed on 24 July, with strong formations escorted by fighters. The Luftwaffe suffered heavily, with fourteen aircraft lost in combat or in accidents, and three more damaged. Fighter Command lost four aircraft, with one pilot rescued from the sea, and six aircraft damaged but repairable. Shipping attacks continued on the next day, coupled with E-boats trying to penetrate the Royal Navy screens near Dover. It was another costly day for the Germans, with nineteen aircraft destroyed in combat or accidents and six more damaged. One of those lost was a Junkers Ju88A of 5./Kampfgeschwader 51 which collided with a Miles Magister trainer near RAF South Cerney in Gloucestershire. Fighter Command did not fare too well with eight aircraft lost,

Bolton Paul Defiant Is had some success in the Battle of France when the Luftwaffe pilots mistook them for Hurricanes, but began to suffer when enemy pilots learnt to attack from head-on or under the belly. They lost heavily in July and August 1940 during the Battle of Britain and were transferred to the role of night-fighters.

Philip Jarrett collection

although two pilots were saved, and ten aircraft damaged but repairable. VIII. Fliegerkorps made attacks on 26 July off the Isle of Wight. In these and other attacks the Germans lost five aircraft, plus five damaged. Fighter Command lost only one aircraft, with five damaged but repairable.

The destroyer HMS *Codrington* was sunk in Dover by air attack on 27 July, while two more destroyers were damaged. This was the first occasion when Messerschmitt Bf109E–4/Bs were employed as fighter-bombers, carrying up to 550lb of bombs under the fuselage. By this time the situation at Dover was considered too perilous for use as a base by the Royal Navy. It had become known as 'Hellfire Corner' by the inventive national press. The Admiralty abandoned the harbour for its anti-invasion measures, although of course the warships continued to escort the convoys. Another destroyer, HMS *Wren*, was sunk off Aldeburgh in Suffolk, while the destroyer HMS *Montrose* was damaged and towed into Harwich Harbour. The Germans lost only four aircraft on this day, with six damaged, while Fighter Command lost two aircraft and two damaged.

In the afternoon of 28 July Spitfires and Hurricanes were involved in air battles with Messerschmitt Bf109s off Dover. Major Werner Mölders was injured in one of these. It was his first operational flight after being appointed commandant of Jagdgeschwader 51 in replacement for Oberst Theo Osterkamp, who took over command of all the fighters and Zerstörer units in Luftflotte 2. His Staffel was engaged by Spitfires of 41 Squadron, and he was hit in the leg while his aircraft was badly damaged. He belly-landed on the French coast and was taken to hospital, then grounded for about a month. The Germans lost eleven aircraft and four more damaged on this day, while Fighter Command lost five aircraft with six damaged but repairable.

Attacks near Dover and Harwich took place on 29 July, with fierce air battles. The Germans lost fourteen aircraft plus six damaged, while Fighter Command's losses were six aircraft plus ten damaged but repairable. The destroyer HMS *Delight* was set on fire by air attack off Portland and sank in harbour the following day. Poor weather restricted activity on 30 July but the attackers still lost nine aircraft plus three damaged, while Fighter Command had one aircraft written off and three damaged but repairable. The last day of the month saw widespread attacks on shipping, with seven German aircraft written off for various reasons, and two damaged. Fighter Command lost two Blenheims which collided with each other, three Spitfires and two Hurricanes destroyed, plus two aircraft damaged but repairable.

August opened with a continuation of the anti-shipping operations, VIII. Fliegerkorps despatching escorted bombers to attack convoys off Hastings. During the night bombers began to drop leaflets with a transcript of Hitler's speech in the Reichstag of 19 July 1940, entitled 'Last Appeal to Reason' and appealing to Britain for a negotiated peace. Civilians read these with a mixture of contempt and amusement. In operations and accidents the attackers lost thirteen aircraft and four damaged, while Fighter Command lost four aircraft plus four more damaged but repairable. The next day, 2 August, brought an attack against a convoy on the east coast. The Luftwaffe lost seven aircraft on operations or in accidents, with nine others damaged. Fighter Command lost three aircraft and two damaged but repairable, all in accidents. This was followed by a relatively quiet day, but the Luftflotten lost six aircraft plus four damaged, while Fighter Command lost two in accidents.

There was a respite on 4 August, mainly confined to German reconnaissance. There were no losses in combats but both sides experienced accidents. The Luftwaffe suffered four aircraft lost and six damaged while Fighter Command lost an aircraft written off and another damaged but repairable. There were some clashes on the following day over the Channel. It was not a good day for the attackers, with eight aircraft lost and thirteen damaged, while the RAF lost one in combat and another accidentally, with four damaged but repairable. There was another respite on 6 August, with all the casualties on both sides caused by a high level of accidents. The attackers lost six aircraft plus seven damaged, while Fighter Command also had six aircraft written off plus two damaged but repairable.

The final day of this first phase of the Battle of Britain, 7 August, was confined to reconnaissance. Yet the Luftwaffe lost two aircraft and ten more damaged, four of the latter in an RAF bombing attack on an airfield. Fighter Command lost five aircraft in accidents, with three more damaged but repairable.

Bomber Command was not inactive in this first phase, with night attacks on ports and airfields in Germany, the Netherlands and Belgium, as well as some minelaying off enemy ports and raids on German industrial centres. There were also daylight raids by Blenheims on ports and airfields in Germany, the Netherlands and France, although the attackers sometimes lost heavily.

The Luftwaffe had suffered considerably in this period, both from combat and accidents. They had sunk about 50,000 tons of shipping, hardly a good return for these losses. However, their major attacks on the British mainland had not yet begun. British Intelligence was aware that the country would be put to a major test, but the date of commencement was uncertain.

Leaflets with verbatim accounts of Hitler's speech to the Reichstag on 19 July 1940, in which he castigated his enemies for failing to make peace with the Third Reich, were dropped over Britain by the Luftwaffe. A milkman in a south-east town who picked up one of them during his early morning rounds on 23 August 1940 evidently found the content very amusing.

Author's collection

Generalfeldmarschall Hugo Sperrle, the commander of Luftflotte 3, with a swagger stick in his right hand, pictured during a visit to II./Kampfgeschwader 27 at its base near Dinard in France during the Battle of Britain. He was 56 years of age at the time. He commanded the Condor Legion in Spain from November 1936 until November 1937, and later took over command of Luftflotte 3, until 21 September 1944. He died in Munich on 7 April 1953.

Jean-Louis Roba collection

Reichsmarschall Hermann Goering on one of his visits to northern France. The man behind his left shoulder is a member of the Reichssicherheitsdienst (German Security Service), who acted as bodyguards or drivers. Born on 12 January 1893 in Bavaria, Goering was an infantry officer on the Western Front in 1914 but obtained his pilot's licence in the autumn of the following year. He became an ace in the German Air Force, was awarded the *Pour le Mérite*, and succeeded Richthofen as commander of the 'Death Squadron'. He joined the Nazi party in 1922, organised the Storm Troopers and founded the Gestapo. He was responsible for developing the Luftwaffe into a major fighting force and became Hitler's successor-designate on the outbreak of war. His star began to fade with the defeat of the Luftwaffe in the Battle of Britain and the Allied bombing of Germany. By 1945 he was in disgrace and fled to Austria, where he was eventually captured by US troops. He was sentenced to death by hanging at Nuremburg but committed suicide on 15 October 1946 before this could be carried out.

Jean-Louis Roba collection

Mechanics working on the Messerschmitt Bf109E-4 of Oberleutnant Bruno Stolle, Staffelkapitän of 8./Jagdgeschwader 2 'Richthofen'. The coat of arms of Oberleutnant von Winterfeld is on the engine cover.

A Messerschmitt Bf110C-4, A2+BB, of I./Zerstörergeschwader 52 on a French airfield during the Blitzkrieg. This unit was renamed II./Zerstörergeschwader 2 in June 1940 and took part in the Battle of Britain.

A Fieseler Fi 156C-1 'Storch' flying out a pilot of a Messerschmitt Bf109 of Jagdgeschwader 2, who had ditched in the Channel during the Battle of Britain. He had been rescued and brought to France. This little aircraft had remarkably short take-off and landing capabilities. It took off almost vertically against a wind of about 25mph. Apart from casualty evacuation, it was used for tactical reconnaissance.

The Heinkel He59 floatplane, designed primarily for reconnaissance and torpedo-bombing, was also employed on air-sea rescue with white livery and Red Cross markings as shown on these He59C-2s. The machine in the foreground, D-ASUO of Seenotflugkommando 1, was forced down on the Goodwin Sands in the evening of 9 July 1940 by Spitfire I serial P9367 of 54 Squadron from Rochford in Essex, flown by Pilot Officer J.L. Allen. It was towed into Ramsgate Harbour by the Walmer lifeboat. The German pilot, Unteroffizier Gunther Maywald, and his crew of three were taken prisoner. On 20 July 1940 the Air Ministry ordered that such aircraft should be shot down, since they were being used for reconnaissance. The He59s were then armed and camouflaged.

Heinkel He59C-2 floatplane, D-AGUI, preparing to pick up men from a dinghy. This was probably a practice exercise.

Some Avro Ansons were still soldiering on with Coastal Command during the Battle of Britain, after their introduction as reconnaissance aircraft in March 1936. They had only a limited range, poor armament and very low bomb-carrying capacity, but they were highly reliable and well-loved by the aircrews. This example was on the strength of 502 Squadron at Aldergrove in Northern Ireland, engaged on convoy escort duties. The squadron was equipped with these machines until November 1940, when it was re-equipped with Whitley Vs.
Author's collection

A field battery in training, preparing to resist any attempt by the Wehrmacht to invade England.
Author's collection

This Heinkel He59 of Seenotflugkommando 1, D-AGIO, was attacked about 20 miles south-east of Start Point in Devon in the morning of 11 July 1940 by an Anson of 217 Squadron flown from St Eval in Cornwall by Sergeant Nelson H. Webb. It was known that these air-sea rescue floatplanes were carrying out reconnaissance duties, and the Air Ministry had warned that they would be attacked. Webb opened fire with his front gun and then banked to allow his gunner in the turret to fire. The Heinkel ditched in the sea and the RAF crew watched while three Germans got into their dinghy, before the machine turned over. They were picked up by a German launch.

Mrs Eunice Godfrey via Graham Pitchfork

A bombing attack on a British convoy off Dover
on 14 July 1940.

Author's collection

The Spitfire excelled in its additional role as a
high-speed and unarmed photo-reconnaissance
aircraft. The first were known as Spitfire PR IAs,
and one of these made the first operational
flight on 18 November 1939, from Seclin in
France over Germany as far as Aachen. Various
marks of this new aircraft were produced,
providing longer ranges or different
combinations of air cameras. This example, serial
N3117, was converted from a PR IB to a PR IE
and fitted with two F24 cameras pointing
outwards for low-level operations. It first flew
on 3 July 1940, and four days later brought back
some excellent photographs of Boulogne from
300ft.

Author's collection

On 21 July 1940 this Messerschmitt Bf110C-5, coded 5F+CM, of Aufklärungsgruppe 4.(F)/14 'Münchhausen-Staffel', was on a reconnaissance sortie over England when it was forced down on Goodwood Home Farm by three Hurricane Is of 238 Squadron based at Middle Wallop in Hampshire. The pilot and navigator were captured. The machine was restored to flying condition with parts from a Messerschmitt Bf110C-4 and given the RAF serial number AX772.

Philip Jarrett collection

In the morning of 24 July 1940 about forty Messerschmitt Bf109s of III./Jagdgeschwader 26, led by Major Adolf Galland, escorted two Staffeln of Dornier Do17s in an attack against a convoy in the Thames estuary. In the ensuing air battle, Messerschmitt Bf109E-1 of Stab III./Jagdgeschwader 26 was shot down by Squadron Leader Henry C. Sawyer in a Spitfire I of 65 Squadron, based at Hornchurch in Essex but operating from Manston in Kent. The pilot was the Geschwader-Adjutant, Oberleutnant Werner Bartels, who was seriously wounded and taken prisoner. His aircraft was later put on display in a municipal car park in Croydon.

Philip Jarrett collection

Three flights of Hurricanes flying below alto-stratus cloud. At the beginning of the Battle of Britain Fighter Command persisted with vics of three, with two in each vic formating on a leader. This was shown to be less effective than the looser 'four-finger' formation developed by Luftwaffe fighter pilots who flew in the Condor Legion during the Spanish Civil War of 1936–9.

Author's collection

Dornier Do17M unit code A5+EA of the Geschwaderstabstaffel of Sturzkampf-geschwader 1, flown by Unteroffizier Lengenbrink, was shot down on 25 July 1940 by Spitfire Is of 152 Squadron based at Warmwell in Dorset, while on a reconnaissance mission. The pilot was killed and the other two crew members were captured, one wounded.

Author's collection

Dover was attacked in the early morning of 29 July 1940 by Ju87 Stukas. Four of the dive-bombers were brought down by anti-aircraft fire and RAF fighters.

Author's collection

A British merchant vessel sinking during an attack by German aircraft in the English Channel in 1940.

J. Falconer collection

Troops of the Indian Army Service Corps, evacuated from Dunkirk, were re-equipped and provided with fresh mules to take part in the defence of Britain. This photograph was taken while a contingent was marching along the coast, led by an Indian piper.

Author's collection

Winston Churchill during a visit to coastal
defence fortifications in Yorkshire on 31 July
1940.

Author's collection

Getting the feel of a 'Tommy' gun after the
mechanism had been described to him.

Author's collection

Winston Churchill under fire. When the Prime Minister visited the Home Guard in a Yorkshire village on 31 July 1940, his party was ambushed by a group of children, one of whom pointed a toy pistol at him. By this time the Home Guard numbered 1,250,000 men throughout the country.

Author's collection

(*Left*) Mrs Winston Churchill dancing with one of the employees of a munitions factory in the north of England. The photograph was taken in a Ministry of Supply hostel, after work. About 140 girls from the south of England were employed at this factory. There seems to have been a shortage of men at the dance.

Author's collection

(Overleaf) 'FIRST ENCOUNTER'
by Mark Postlethwaite
Sergeant Gordon Batt in a Hurricane of 238 Squadron, based at Middle Wallop in Hampshire, meets a German aircraft for the first time in July 1940 – a head-on encounter with a Messerschmitt Bf110 over Chesil Beach in Dorset.

Women workers in an ordnance factory helping
to increase the output of guns.

Author's collection

Messerschmitt Bf109E-4s of III./Jagdgeschwader 27 (formerly Jagdgeschwader I) being refuelled in mid-1940 at an airfield near Carquebut in France. The fuselage access panel of the nearest aircraft has been removed. The two pilots are wearing different types of lifejacket. This unit went on a refresher course in the autumn of 1940 and participated in the campaign in the Balkans during the following spring.

Philip Jarrett collection

Bombs exploding off Dover Harbour.

Bruce Robertson collection

Messerschmitt Bf109E-1s of III./Jagdgeschwader 52, which was stationed in the Pas de Calais from the end of July for a few weeks. The unit can be identified by the wavy lines behind the Balkenkreuz (German cross). The aircraft are fitted with 57mm bullet-resistant armoured glass in front of the windscreens. This unit was transferred in October 1940 to an airfield near Kabarcie in Romania.

Philip Jarrett collection

A Messerschmitt Bf109E-4 of III./Jagdgeschwader 52 on standby in France at the end of July 1940. The 57mm bullet-resistant windscreen and the inertia starting handle can be seen in the photograph.

The Focke-Wulf Fw200 Condor, adapted from a 26-seat commercial airliner, became a formidable anti-shipping aircraft. It operated from French and Norwegian bases over the Atlantic and the waters of north-east Europe, often in conjunction with U-boats. With a long range and a heavy bomb-load, it was responsible for sinking many Allied merchant vessels. The example here is a Focke-Wulf Fw200C-3.

Author's collection

This Focke-Wulf Fw200C-3 Condor, on the strength of Kampfgeschwader 40, was photographed at Brest in 1940.

Several of these Breguet 521 Bizerte flying boats were captured by the Germans after the fall of France and were employed on air-sea rescue from French seaplane bases during the Battle of Britain. This example, radio code KD+BA, was on the strength of 1.Seenotstaffel stationed at Brest. One of these tri-motored machines was recaptured after D-Day and found to be still serviceable.

Volunteer Underwood taking her first driving lesson in a heavy Army lorry, instructed by a soldier of the Royal Engineers.

Author's collection

CHAPTER FIVE

BEGINNING OF THE MAIN ASSAULT

On 31 July 1940 the commander of the Kriegsmarine, Admiral Erich Raeder, advised Hitler that the seaborne part of Operation Sealion could not be launched until the middle of September. Even then a successful invasion of Britain would depend on whether the Luftwaffe succeeded in establishing air superiority over the RAF. Moreover, substantial damage would have to be inflicted on the enemy from the air during the first fortnight of the operation, so that waves of reinforcements and supplies could be brought over without great hindrance. If these objectives could not be achieved, the invasion would have to be delayed until the next spring.

On the following day Hitler ordered Goering to 'destroy the English Air Force as soon as possible'. He suggested 5 August as the possible date for the beginning of a great air assault, but left the final choice with Goering. He also ordered his army commanders to continue their preparations so as to be ready for the invasion by the middle of September.

Hitler had named Field Marshal Hermann Goering as his successor in the event of his death, when addressing the Reichstag on 1 September 1939, the day of the invasion of Poland. Goering had thus become the Deputy Führer while the previous nominee, Rudolf Hess, had been relegated to third place. The head of the Luftwaffe was a popular figure in Germany, well-liked for his achievements as a flier in the First World War and for the bonhomie and confidence he exuded. His extravagant and self-indulgent life-style was either overlooked or considered not detrimental to a man in his position. He was hailed as the 'Iron Man' in charge of the largest and most effective air force in the world.

Unfortunately for the Luftwaffe, their bombastic and forceful chief was not over-blessed with intelligence, nor was he particularly well served by those responsible for feeding him with information about the RAF. Combat reports from pilots and aircrews in the anti-shipping attacks over the English Channel had led to the belief that far more RAF aircraft had been shot down than was the case. It was estimated that Fighter Command had been reduced to about 675 aircraft, whereas the true figure was roughly 1,000, of which about about 750 were normally serviceable. Production of new fighters was believed to be about 200 a month, whereas the true figure was nearer 600, if repaired aircraft were taken into account.

Goering believed that his Luftwaffe could destroy Fighter Command in the south of England within four days and eliminate the whole of the RAF in four weeks, partly by bombing airfields and factories. On 3 August he convened a small conference of senior Luftwaffe officers at Karinhall, his luxurious estate 40 miles north-east of Berlin, in which some preliminary problems were thrashed out. This was followed by another meeting at Karinhall on 6 August, attended by all three commanders of Luftflotten 2, 3 and 5, for a final briefing. Both Galland and Mölders were present, and each was invested with the Pilot's Badge in Gold, with Diamonds. However, they were told that the fighter arm was providing insufficient protection for the bombers. Goering wanted more aggression and promoted each to Oberst, convinced that younger men were the answer to any problems. Behind Goering's thinking was his assumption that Germans were a race of warriors, whereas the English were tradesmen, Anglo-Saxons grown soft from living off the spoils of their empire. A date was set for the main assault to begin, 10 August, provided the weather was favourable. It was given the rather grandiose title *Adler Tag* (Eagle Day).

A day after this conference a German intelligence appreciation of Fighter Command's control system was circulated. As shown in the following extract, it is evident that these specialists still knew little of the centralised organisation at Bentley Priory built up by Dowding:

> As the British fighters are controlled from the ground by their R/T their forces are tied to their respective ground stations and are thereby restricted in mobility, even taking into account the probability that their ground stations are partly mobile. Consequently, the assembly of strong fighter forces at determined points and at short notice is not to be expected. . . . It can, indeed, be assumed that considerable confusion in the defensive networks will be unavoidable during mass attacks, and that the effectiveness of the defences may therefore be reduced.

By this time the total strength of the three Luftflotten facing Britain was about 3,350 bombers, fighters and reconnaissance aircraft. These constituted about 70 per cent of the total front-line strength of the Luftwaffe throughout Europe. The other were Luftflotte 1 facing Russia and Luftflotte 4 facing the south-east and the Balkans. However, all aircraft needed regular maintenance and overhaul, so that only about three-quarters of these numbers were serviceable at any one time.

The Germans were not fully aware that Dowding had been husbanding his resources and even building up his strength. His squadrons now numbered fifty-five, with six more nearing completion of their training. He had over 1,400 pilots, including those shot down during the previous few weeks who had returned to their units, with more coming through the training system. Among the newcomers were experienced pilots from the USA who had joined the RAF and converted on to its machines. Others were Polish and Czechoslovakian pilots who had improved their English enough to cope with the R/T and learnt how to fly Hurricanes; these were numerous enough to form their own squadrons, with an equivalent number of RAF pilots in the first few months. Volunteer pilots from many European and other countries were anxious to join in the fight against the menace of National Socialism. The whole of the RAF was rapidly

President Eduard Benes of Czechoslovakia visited RAF Honington in Suffolk on 6 August 1940. This was the base for 311 (Czech) Squadron, which had been formed with Wellington IAs on 29 July 1940.

Author's collection

becoming a cosmopolitan organisation. But the fighting of the next few weeks drew heavily on the resources of Fighter Command.

Strong attacks against a convoy took place off the south coast on 8 August, with Stukas from VIII. Fliegerkorps escorted by Bf109s and Bf110s. Major air battles ensued, with the Spitfire pilots of No. 11 Group under orders to engage the Messerschmitt escorts so far as possible while the Hurricane pilots tackled the bombers. Some Stukas got through, sinking four merchant ships and damaging several more. There were heavy losses in the resulting air battles. During this and other encounters on the same day, the Germans lost twenty-four aircraft with twenty-five damaged. Fighter Command lost twenty aircraft plus eleven damaged but repairable. This was the worst day for the RAF to date in the Battle of Britain. The losses also demonstrated the inadequacy of the RAF's air-sea rescue service, for only one injured pilot was brought back from the sea, by an escort vessel. The Germans, who were far better organised with floatplanes and launches, managed to rescue three pilots.

The following day was the intended eve of *Adler Tag* and there was less activity while the Luftflotten were making their preparations. They lost only six aircraft in operations or accidents, plus four more damaged. Fighter Command lost two aircraft in accidents plus four damaged in combat or accidents but repairable. But bad weather was forecast and the great German assault scheduled for the next day was deferred to await better flying conditions. Thus the lull continued for the next two days but three German aircraft did not return from operations, five were written off in accidents and eleven were damaged for various reasons. Fighter Command lost three aircraft in accidents, while seven were damaged in combat or accidents but repairable.

The weather on 11 August was still cloudy but there was far more activity, even though Goering had deferred *Adler Tag* for two more days. Attacks by large formations took place over both the Dover and Portland areas. Two ships were sunk off the latter area and fierce air battles raged over the Channel. Lufflotten 2 and 3 lost thirty-eight aircraft destroyed and sixteen damaged during the day, although the German air-sea rescue picked up five fighter pilots and the entire crew of a Junkers Ju88. Fighter Command's losses were also extremely heavy, with twenty-seven aircraft shot down and eighteen damaged but repairable.

The nose of a Junkers Ju88A on the strength of one of the three Gruppen of Kampfgeschwader 30, also known as the 'Adler Geschwader', stationed at Aalborg in Denmark during August 1940. Note the additional armament mounted in one of the perspex panels.

Georges Van Acker collection

This pace continued on the next day. The Luftflotten struck their first major blows against airfields and RDF stations in Kent, Sussex and the Isle of Wight. They lost thirty-two aircraft during the day, as well as eighteen damaged, but some of their bombing was effective. The most serious loss for the RAF was the almost total destruction of the RDF station at Ventnor in the Isle of Wight, which was dive-bombed by Junkers Ju88s. Although a mobile station was brought in to keep the chain of RDF stations intact, it was feared that this might be a prelude to more sustained attacks, constituting a grave blow to the whole defence system. But this did not happen, partly because the Luftwaffe chiefs still did not understand the importance of these stations and partly because it was difficult to dive-bomb these stations without crashing into the tall masts. Nevertheless, German propaganda asserted that the day was a great success, with airfields put out of action and eighty fighters destroyed. In fact, Fighter Command lost seventeen aircraft during the day plus thirty damaged but repairable.

These exaggerated claims of enemy aircraft destroyed continued by all sides throughout the war. To some extent they were the result of genuine beliefs on the part of those making them. Combats usually lasted only a few seconds in confusing circumstances, and a pilot or air gunner who saw an enemy aircraft going down could easily assume that it was the one he had fired at. 'Double counting' or even multiple counting occurred on frequent occasions. Moreover smoke from an exhaust could be mistaken for smoke from an engine on fire, while the pilot or gunner could seldom follow the aircraft down to see whether it crashed. When the crews were debriefed, squadron intelligence officers were eager to learn of their prowess, and forwarded glowing reports to headquarters. High commanders released the figures to journalists for propaganda reasons. However, the German commanders seem to have believed such reports without question, and made their calculations and plans accordingly. Dowding had a far

This Dornier Do17Z unit code U5+DS of 8./Kampfgeschwader 2 'Holzhammer' was shot down on 13 August 1940 by Hurricane Is of 111 Squadron based at Croydon, while on a bombing mission against RAF Eastchurch in Kent. It crashed on mudflats at Seesalter near Whitstable in Kent. One of the crew was killed and the other three captured.

Author's collection

better appreciation of the true figures from the number of enemy aircraft known to have crashed in England, and in any case was a more cautious commander.

German intelligence officers also underestimated the capacity of the RAF and civilian workers to repair the damage done to airfields. In fact craters in airfields were rapidly filled in and the stations were at least partly back in action during the next day. When this day dawned, on 13 August, Goering's *Adler Tag* had at last arrived. It was the first day of the great assault which would eliminate the aircraft of Fighter Command and pulverise the airfields and aircraft factories. Then Operation Sealion would follow. However, the day was marked by confusion and muddle on the part of the attackers. Goering had decided once more that *Adler Tag* should be deferred, this time to await clearer weather in the afternoon, but some formations were already airborne. Meanwhile, the Government Code and Cypher School at Bletchley Park had picked up and decyphered this code-name but did not know what it meant.

Two formations of Dornier Do17s and Messerschmitt Bf110s from Luftflotte 2 were in the air. One headed for RAF Eastchurch in Kent, under the false impression that it was a fighter airfield, whereas it actually came under Coastal Command's No. 16 Group and housed some Blenheims on detachment. The target of the other formation was the harbour at Sheerness in Kent. The Bf110s received a recall and turned for home but the Do17s carried on unescorted. Both formations were intercepted by fighters, and some of the rear aircraft were chopped out of the sky. Nevertheless, Eastchurch was accurately bombed, with buildings and some Blenheims destroyed. The bombs intended for Sheerness were jettisoned into the sea during the air combats.

Two other formations, both from Luftflotte 3 and escorted by fighters, headed over Sussex to attack the Royal Aircraft Establishment at Farnborough and the nearby RAF airfield at Odiham. They were intercepted as soon as they crossed the coast and all missed their targets. Another formation from Luftflotte 3 approached in the afternoon from the direction of Cherbourg. This turned out to consist of Messerschmitt Bf110s which had failed to rendezvous with the bombers they were supposed to escort. They lost heavily from the attentions of two RAF squadrons. Three waves of Junkers Ju87s and Ju88s from Luftflotte 3 followed, heading towards Southampton and escorted by Messerschmitt Bf109s. These were hotly engaged by Hurricanes and Spitfires, but much damage was done in Southampton. The Ju87s bombed RAF Andover, causing little damage, but missed their main target of RAF Middle Wallop. They suffered especially badly from RAF fighters.

Luftflotte 2 also despatched waves of bombers and fighters in the afternoon. The fighter airfields of Detling in Kent and Southend in Essex with its satellite of Rochford were their main targets, but thick cloud in this area hindered navigation and bombing. There was heavy fighting but Detling was severely hit while the airfields in Essex were missed entirely and the bombs were jettisoned near Canterbury.

The day ended with a clear victory for Fighter Command, which lost fourteen aircraft. Ten pilots survived, since most of the battles had taken place over land, but some of them were injured. Eighteen other aircraft were damaged but repairable. *Adler Tag* cost the Luftflotten thirty-nine aircraft lost in operations or accidents, plus forty-seven damaged, many struggling home with injured aircrew. German propaganda trumpeted the day as a great success, with hugely exaggerated claims of RAF aircraft destroyed, while the military marching song *Bomben auf England* was played repeatedly over the wireless to an ecstatic public. The empty places around the mess tables in the operational airfields told a different story.

The German effort on the next day was far smaller, beginning with a bombing attack by Messerschmitt Bf110s on RAF Manston in Kent, escorted by Bf109s. Thick cloud covered their approach and four hangars were hit, although ground gunners accounted for two of the Bf110s. Another formation approached Dover, shot down seven barrage balloons and dropped a few bombs. A succession of attacks on airfields and towns in the south followed from Luftflotte 3, causing some damage and the blockage of a railway line near Southampton. The day cost the Luftflotten twenty aircraft destroyed and seven damaged; Fighter Command lost six aircraft in combat, three Blenheims destroyed on the ground at Manston and eleven aircraft damaged for various reasons. In the past week the number of Fighter Command's aircraft lost or put out of action had exceeded the flow of new machines coming from the factories and the repair organisations, but the majority of the damaged aircraft were capable of repair and would eventually reappear.

Extremely heavy attacks were made on the next day, 15 August. Over 1,750 sorties were flown by all three Luftflotten in coordinated daylight operations, designed to spread Fighter Command's resources beyond their limit. They began at about 11.00 hours when a formation of some forty Stukas, strongly escorted by Bf109s, attacked the airfields of Hawkinge and Lympne in Kent. Spitfires and Hurricanes took a heavy toll but some Stukas got through and caused quite heavy damage, including the cutting of power lines to three RDF stations.

In the late morning Luftflotte 5 despatched about sixty-five Heinkel He111 bombers of Kampfgeschwader 26, escorted by about thirty Bf110D-1/R1s of Zerstörergeschwader 76 from Stavanger in Norway, to attack targets in north-east England. These were in two formations. To increase their range, each Bf110 long-range fighter was fitted with a non-jettisonable auxiliary tank named a

Barrage balloons were fairly easy targets for Messerschmitt Bf109s. This balloon was brought down in flames over Dover in Kent on 14 August 1940.

Author's collection

Four Junkers Ju87B dive-bombers of 3./Stukageschwader 2 'Immelmann' were shot down on 16 August 1940 during an attack on Tangmere airfield in Sussex. A group of interested civilians is examining one of these, coded T6+HL, which came down beside the Selsey–Chichester road. Children cycled from miles around to look at such strange foreign objects. Crashed enemy aircraft were officially regarded as good publicity, but the remains of downed RAF fighters were quickly cleared away and private photography was prohibited.

Philip Jarrett collection

Dackelbauch ('Dachshund belly') under the fuselage. This was divided into four compartments containing the explosive mixture of 1,010 litres of petrol and 80 litres of oil. Fumes remained in this lethal tank even when it was empty, and a single bullet could blow the aircraft to bits. Seven of these machines failed to return when they were tackled by about forty Hurricanes and Spitfires of No. 13 Group, which picked them off when they went into their usual defensive circles. The Heinkels scattered and eight were shot down while others jettisoned their bombs over the sea. Some reached the coast and dropped their bombs but with little effect. Not a single RAF fighter was lost.

Another formation from Luftflotte 5, based at Aalborg in Denmark, consisted of about fifty Junkers Ju88s which headed towards Yorkshire. These were also intercepted but some got through. The main force bombed Bomber Command's station at Driffield, destroying ten Whitleys and damaging hangars while one was shot down by ground defence. Six of these Ju88s failed to return, while Fighter Command lost none. Luftflotte 5 never again attempted mass daylight attacks after this disastrous day.

Further south Stukas escorted by Bf110s slipped through the defences and attacked the fighter airfield of Martlesham Heath in Suffolk, causing damage and escaping before Hurricanes and Spitfires arrived. Another strong force of bombers flew up the Thames estuary while their fighters held off the RAF. They bombed the Short factory at Rochester, causing delays in the production of Stirling bombers. Other formations of Junkers Ju88s escorted by Bf110s, from Luftflotte 3, flew over the Isle of Wight to attack the fighter airfield at Middle Wallop and the maintenance base of Worthy Down, both in Hampshire. They were continually harried by RAF fighters. In the early evening formations from Luftflotte 2 heading for fighter airfields in Kent were broken up and achieved little.

It had been a hard day for both sides but especially severe for the three Luftflotten. During the day and in some subsequent night attacks they lost seventy-seven aircraft plus twenty-one damaged. By comparison, Fighter Command lost thirty-two aircraft plus two Blenheims destroyed on the ground, with twenty-eight fighters damaged but repairable.

It became evident to the Luftwaffe High Command that *Adler Tag* and the two following days had gone badly. Some of the commanders began to doubt the accuracy of an Intelligence assessment, which had worked out a figure of about 300 aircraft for the remaining strength of Fighter Command. But they still did not appreciate the vital importance of the British RDF system. Goering continued to blame his fighter force for not giving enough protection to the bombers, especially the vulnerable Stuka dive-bombers. No doubt influenced by complaints from the crews, he ordered that three fighters should escort each bomber in future. It is strange that this fighter pilot from the First World War did not understand the folly of compelling fighters to weave in close proximity to the bombers. Although their presence gave visual comfort to the bomber crews, such tactics were far less effective than attaining altitude and then diving down on enemy fighters.

The situation in Fighter Command was far less parlous than the Germans believed. Taking into account the Blenheim, Gladiator and Defiant squadrons, Dowding still had a total of 672 aircraft, of which 570 were Hurricanes and Spitfires. The high losses of aircraft and damage to others were depleting reserve stocks but it was estimated that at the existing rate of output the battle could be sustained for two more months. The depleted number of pilots was far more worrying. About seventy new pilots were arriving through the training system each week, but those on the squadrons were being killed or injured at a higher rate. Dowding asked the Air Ministry if some of the experienced pilots in the four Bomber Command squadrons still equipped with the obsolete Fairey Battles could be transferred. This was at first refused, on the grounds that these Battles might be required to attack an invasion force, but two days later it was accepted. Five volunteers from each Battle squadron began a quick conversion course, as well as three volunteers from each of the eleven Army Co-operation squadrons. Thus fifty-three replacement pilots became available within a week, in addition to the seventy from the Operational Training Units.

The damage to airfields was also causing concern. On 16 August Lympne, West Malling and Croydon were struggling to restore their services, and it seemed certain that other attacks on airfields would follow. This fear was justified when enemy aircraft began to pour over towards Kent. The RAF airfields of West Malling and Manston were hit while as usual Fighter Command took its toll of the attackers. Other formations headed for the Thames estuary, Dover and the south coast. In spite of air battles, they caused damage to London suburbs, the Fleet Air Arm base at Lee-on-Solent, RAF Tangmere in Sussex, and the Royal Aircraft Establishment's base at Farnborough in Hampshire. An effective raid was carried out in the afternoon against the maintenance and training base of Brize Norton in Oxfordshire. The day cost the Luftflotten forty-four aircraft destroyed and twenty-four damaged. Including aircraft damaged on the ground by air attack, Fighter Command suffered twenty-four aircraft written off and eighteen damaged but repairable.

(*Overleaf*) Pilots of 32 Squadron photographed in July 1940 at Hawkinge in Kent, in front of one of their Hurricane Is. Left to right: Pilot Officer R.F. Smythe, Pilot Officer K.R. Gillman, Pilot Officer J.E. Proctor, Flight Lieutenant P.M. Brothers, Pilot Officer D.H. Grice, Pilot Officer D.M. Gardner and Pilot Officer A.F. Eckford. Gillman lost his life in combat on 25 August 1940, but the others survived the Battle of Britain.

Author's collection

This picture of two German crew members boarding a military transport was taken in an 'English coastal town, watched by a crowd of curious villagers', by an American photographer during the Battle of Britain. The original caption stated that they were two members of a crew of five rescued uninjured from an aircraft shot down in the sea. The Heinkel He111 carried a crew of five.

A Speech by
The Prime Minister

THE RIGHT HONOURABLE

WINSTON CHURCHILL

in the House of Commons

AUGUST 20th, 1940

J. Falconer collection

Fighter Command's only Victoria Cross of the war was awarded to a pilot for an action on this day. In the early afternoon Flight Lieutenant James B. Nicolson of 249 Squadron took off from Boscombe Down in Wiltshire, flying Hurricane 1 serial P3576. He was an experienced pilot but this was to be his first combat, leading Red Section towards Gosport. The three Hurricanes were attacked by Bf109s and all were hit. One pilot baled out but was killed when his parachute was shredded by fire from the ground. Another pilot crash-landed back at Boscombe Down. The gravity tank in Nicolson's Hurricane was set on fire while cannon shells wounded him in the left foot and tore his left eyelid. He prepared to bale out but a Messerschmitt Bf110 appeared ahead and he opened fire while the flames were scorching him. When he eventually baled out, he was hit in the buttocks during the descent by a Home Guard who fired a shotgun at him. His wounds healed slowly and he returned to active service, only to be killed as a supernumerary observer in a Liberator of 355 Squadron in the Bay of Bengal on 2 May 1945.

This was also the day when Churchill visited the headquarters of Air Vice-Marshal Keith Park's No. 11 Group at Uxbridge in Middlesex and heard the dramatic R/T exchanges between the controllers and the fighter pilots during their air combats. He was accompanied by his military secretary, Major-General Hastings Ismay, who recalled that when they left by car for Chequers, Churchill said: 'Don't speak to me; I have never been so moved in all my life.' Five minutes later, the Prime Minister leaned forward and said: 'Never in the field of human conflict has so much been owed by so many to so few.' This was the superb description of the Battle of Britain which he repeated in the House of Commons in his review of the war four days later. It was carried throughout the free world.

In spite of good weather, there was a lull on 17 August when the Luftflotten gave their crews some respite. The day was confined to reconnaissance flights, followed by some scattered night raids on industrial centres in South Wales, Merseyside and the Midlands. Nevertheless, five aircraft were lost on operations and accidents, with another damaged. Fighter Command lost a Blenheim and a Hurricane in flying accidents, with another Hurricane damaged but repairable.

The following day, 18 August, has been justly described as 'the hardest day'. Huge formations of enemy aircraft from Luftflotte 2 crossed south-east England to make low- and medium-level attacks against the airfields of Biggin Hill and West Malling in Kent, as well as Kenley and Croydon in Surrey. They were intercepted by the RAF but inevitably some got through, to be met by barrages from gun emplacements and 'parachute and cable' devices fired from the airfields. Kenley was badly hit, with buildings and aircraft destroyed, putting the airfield out of action temporarily. The other airfields were also hit, although less severely. Luftflotte 3 concentrated on the south coast, hitting Coastal Command's station of Thorney Island in Hampshire and the Fleet Air Arm's station of Ford in Sussex. The RDF station at Poling, near Chichester, was badly damaged but replaced temporarily by a mobile station. Luftflotte 2 then put in another appearance and attacked Manston and Croydon once more. During the night there were scattered bombing attacks against industrial targets.

The Luftflotten lost sixty-seven aircraft while thirty-five more were damaged. The aircraft which suffered relatively the worst were the Stukas, for seventeen were shot down. This rate of attrition was unbearable and they were grounded. Dive-bombing was a very accurate form of low-level attack, for with a little practice the pilot could place his bomb within a few feet of the target. Moreover the delayed-action bomb struck nose down, ensuring that the exploding mechanism was activated and that the bomb went off a few seconds after the aircraft cleared the area of blast. Bombs dropped from level flight at low altitude could overshoot or undershoot and might even skid over the ground. But the Stukas were slow and had little defence against fighters. They also made excellent targets for ground gunners provided they kept their nerve, for little deflection shooting was required at point-blank range against an aircraft coming almost directly at them. All the Stukas remaining in Luftflotte 3 were transferred to Luftflotte 2. They were intended to revert to their more accustomed role as mobile artillery for assault troops, during an invasion that was still expected.

Fighter Command lost thirty-six aircraft on 18 August, three of which were destroyed on the ground, plus twenty-two damaged but repairable. Ten pilots were killed and twenty-seven injured, some seriously. Both sides drew back from this intense pace for the next few days. A new phase of the battle was about to begin.

A Junkers Ju87B-1 of 3./Sturzkampfgeschwader making its last dive on 18 August 1940, after an attack by Hurricanes over RAF Thorney Island in Hampshire. It crashed at Whitehouse Farm, West Broyle, Chichester, killing the pilot. The observer/gunner seems to have baled out but his body was never recovered. This was one of eighteen dive-bombers shot down in action or crashed back in France on this day. The type was consequently withdrawn from the Battle of Britain.

Author's collection

Air Chief Marshal Sir Keith Park, who was born in 1892 in New Zealand, earned a reputation as one of the finest fighter leaders in the Second World War. He came to Britain to serve as a gunner in the First World War but transferred to the RFC in 1917, being awarded both the MC and the DFC. Between the wars, he commanded RAF squadrons, passed through the RAF Staff College and was appointed as air attaché in Buenos Aires. In 1938 he served as Senior Air Staff Officer under Dowding in Fighter Command. In April 1940, when an Air Vice-Marshal, he was appointed as Air Officer Commanding No. 11 Group, which bore the brunt of the fighting in the Battle of Britain. He then commanded No. 23 Training Group from December 1941 but was posted to the Middle East and served as Air Officer Commanding Egypt, then Malta from July 1942 during the height of the Axis attacks. He was Air Officer Commander-in-Chief Middle East from January 1944 and Allied Air Officer Commander-in-Chief of South-East Asia from February 1945. He died in New Zealand on 5 February 1975.

Author's collection

Air Chief Marshal Sir Trafford L. Leigh-Mallory, photographed with King George VI and Winston Churchill. His experience went back to the First World War, when he commanded 8 Squadron. He commanded the RAF's No. 12 Group as an Air Vice-Marshal during the Battle of Britain, and then No. 11 Group. He commanded Fighter Command as an Air Marshal from 28 November 1942, and then the Allied Expeditionary Air Force from 15 November 1943, as an Air Chief Marshal. He was appointed to command the Allied Air Forces in South-East Asia, but the Avro York which took off from Northolt on 14 November 1944, carrying him, his wife and his staff officer, crashed near Grenoble in bad weather. All on board were killed.

Bruce Robertson collection

An ATS girl at a gun site during the Blitz, receiving and then transmitting messages to the officer in charge.

Author's collection

Hurricane Is of 504 (County of Nottingham) Squadron fought in the latter part of the Battle of Britain, after being based in Scotland on defensive duties. This photograph was taken against a background of strato-cumulus clouds.

J. Falconer collection

Spitfire Is peeling off to attack in line astern.

Bruce Robertson collection

A Heinkel He111P-1 of Kampfgeschwader 55 undergoing service of its Daimler-Benz DB601Aa engines, on a French airfield during the Battle of Britain.

Aircrews of III./Kampfgeschwader 2 'Holzhammer' eating soup from billycans while sitting on bombs in front of their Dornier Do17Zs at Cambrai in France during the Battle of Britain. They are wearing their flying kits and lifejackets ready for take-off.

Groundcrews, with rifles piled at the ready, pictured on an airfield near Devres in the Pas de Calais in early August 1940. Behind them is a Messerschmitt Bf109E-4 of III./Jagdgeschwader 2 'Richthofen'.

Philip Jarrett collection

Hurricane Is of 257 Squadron taking off. The squadron first received these fighters in June 1940.

Aeroplane

No. 1 (RCAF) Squadron was equipped with Hurricane Is from 21 June 1940. The pilots were credited with many victories in the Battle of Britain, and three were awarded Distinguished Flying Crosses.

Author's collection

The view from the nose of a Heinkel He111, with the pilot on the port side. The navigator/bomb aimer usually sat on his folding seat to the starboard, from where he could sit or lie in front of his bombsight or else man the 7.9mm machine-gun in the nose. The radio operator/dorsal gunner could stand behind both men or sit on a cradle seat in his turret, while the ventral gunner lay on a horizontal pad behind his machine-gun.

Philip Jarrett collection

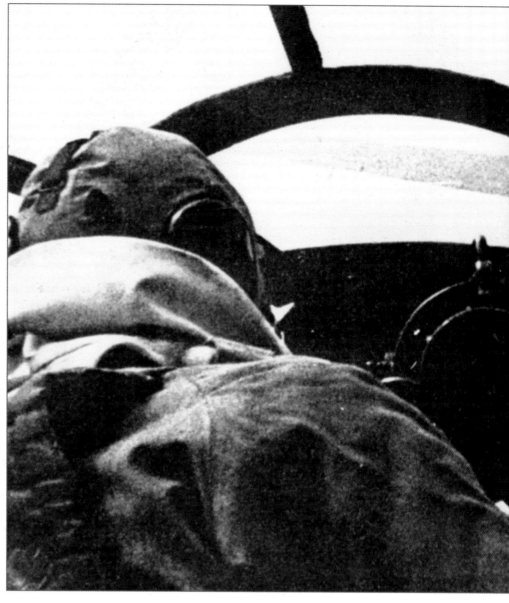

A casualty caused by production shortages during the Battle of Britain was the Spitfire III. This prototype, serial N3297, was first flown by the test pilot Geoffrey Quill on 16 March 1940. It was powered by a Merlin XX engine of 1,390hp and fitted with a two-speed supercharger to provide improved performance at all altitudes. However, insufficient engines were available and the Hurricane II was given priority. Before production could be increased, the Merlin 45 engine was developed and this was installed in the Spitfire V. Production of the Spitfire III never went ahead.

Author's collection

The Heinkel He111 had had a successful career in the Condor Legion during the Spanish Civil War, when it could outrun the existing fighters, but suffered badly in combat with Hurricanes and Spitfires during the Battle of Britain. Armament and crew members were increased for additional defence.

Philip Jarrett collection

Air observers of an RCAF squadron equipped with Lysanders, at practice on the butts with twin Browning .303in machine-guns. They were probably serving with 110 (RCAF) Squadron, based at Old Sarum in Wiltshire from February 1940 and then at Odiham in Hampshire from 9 June 1940 until 1 March 1941.

Author's collection

Pilots of 601 (City of London) Squadron, in front of one of their Hurricane Is showing the squadron's distinctive winged sword emblem on the fin. The squadron was engaged in the Battle of Britain from airfields in the south-east, south and south-west of England. At the time this photograph was taken, ten of the pilots had been awarded the Distinguished Flying Cross.
Author's collection

Pilots and ground mechanics of 610 (County of Chester) Squadron at Biggin Hill in Kent, discussing events beside their Spitfire Is after an air battle in July 1940.

Author's collection

Lieutenant-General Harold Alexander, General Officer Commander-in-Chief of Southern Command from 1940 to 1942, pointing out a shell in flight to King George VI at a forward observation post during training, while Queen Elizabeth covers her ears from the crash of gunfire.

Author's collection

Vapour trails in the sky over Kent during the height of the Battle of Britain.

A Heinkel He111 being lifted from the sea by a patrol vessel during the Battle of Britain, in order to find out its unit and details of construction and equipment. Such wrecks then provided scrap metal for the British armament industry.

TEMPER DASH with DISCRETION

Don't let your eagerness spoil a combined
attack and incidentally make you a 'sitter'
for the enemy.

Royal Air Force Museum AD1305.

(*Right*) Pressing propellant into cartridge cases in a shell-filling factory.

Author's collection

(*Previous page*) Hurricane Is of 32 Squadron at
Biggin Hill in Kent. During the Battle of Britain
the robust and well-loved Hurricanes shot down
more enemy aircraft than all other fighters
combined with the whole of the ground
defences.

Author's collection

Junkers Ju88-A5 unit code 3Z+EP of 6./Kampfgeschwader 77 crashed at Godstone in Surrey during the night of 28/29 November 1940. The crew baled over Reims but the aircraft flew back to England and glided down to crash near a spot where Junkers Ju88A-1 unit code 9K+CL of 3./Kampfgeschwader 51 had crashed on 12 August 1940.

Author's collection

A Spitfire of 19 Squadron at Fowlmere in Cambridgeshire, being re-armed.

Bruce Robertson collection

This faked photograph purports to show a gun camera shot from a Messerschmitt Bf109E of a Spitfire going down on fire. In fact this is a captured Spitfire fitted with smoke generators near the wing roots, giving the appearance of flames. It would have landed safely after this 'combat'.

Bruce Robertson collection

Le Ju 88 le bombardier de vol horizontal et de vol en piqué le plus moderne de notre aviation

The German magazine *Signal* was published by Deutscher Verlag in Berlin, first appearing in mid-1940. It carried articles by war correspondents extolling the victories of the German armed forces. Versions were printed in German, French, Flemish and German–English, and distributed in Belgium, Bohemia-Moravia, Bulgaria, Denmark, Estonia, Finland, France, Germany, Greece, Hungary, Italy, Luxembourg, the Netherlands, Norway, Portugal, Romania, Slovakia, Spain, Sweden, Switzerland, Turkey and the United States up to mid-1941. The final edition appeared in early 1945.

Georges Van Acker collection

'DORNIERS OVER KENLEY'
by Mark Postlethwaite
Dornier Do17Zs of Kampfgeschwader 76,
escorted by Messerschmitt Bf109s, making a
low-level attack against RAF Kenley in Surrey on
18 August 1940.

Spitfire Is of 616 Squadron landing at Leconfield in Yorkshire, where they were based from 6 June to 19 August 1940. The squadron participated in the destruction of six of the Junkers Ju88Cs of Kampfgeschwader 30, Luftflotte 5, from Aalborg in Denmark which were sent on 15 August 1940 to attack the Bomber Command airfield at Driffield.

Graham Pitchfork collection

Dornier Do17Z-2 unit code F1+DT of 9./Kampfgeschwader 76 was flown by the Staffelkäpitan, Hauptmann Roth, on 18 August 1940. Hit by ground fire from RAF Kenley in Surrey and further damaged by Hurricanes of 111 Squadron from RAF Croydon, it crash-landed at Leaves Green near Biggin Hill in Kent. All five crew members got out and were captured and the machine burnt out.

Author's collection

The final dive of a Dornier Do17Z-2 with its starboard engine on fire, photographed from the ground on 18 August 1940. It was probably one of the Dorniers of 9./Kampfgeschwader 76 which were shot down on that day during their attack on Kenley airfield.

Author's collection

CHAPTER SIX

THE MOST DANGEROUS PHASE

Both sides reviewed the progress of the battle on 19 August and issued new instructions. Goering decided that Luftflotte 5 should relinquish its mass raids in daylight and prepare for night raids against Glasgow and other targets in the north of Britain. However, some raids might be made in daylight by single aircraft or small formations using cloud cover. Luftflotten 2 and 3 were to continue weakening Fighter Command in daylight, with the bombers being used primarily as bait to bring the pilots to battle. Both were to make preparations for night attacks on London or Liverpool but these were not to be implemented without his authority. Night raids on other targets could be made at the discretion of the commanders.

In No. 11 Group Air Vice-Marshal Keith Park was concerned about the loss of his pilots incurred in fighter versus fighter combats. He ordered his sector commanders and controllers to concentrate on the bombers as far as possible. With some losses occurring from ditchings in the sea and the inadequate rescue service, he gave orders that pilots were not to engage the enemy beyond gliding range of the coast. He also ordered additional protection for the airfields, telling his controllers to request help from No. 12 Group to guard those north of the Thames if necessary.

Dowding refused Park's request for the transfer of some of the best pilots from less active groups to replace his newcomers. Instead, he adopted the policy of rotating whole squadrons by giving them spells away from No. 11 Group in quieter groups. This must have been based on his experience in the First World War. All pilots engaged in combat with the Luftwaffe in No. 11 Group, experienced or otherwise, were flying with great intensity, sometimes as many as four sorties a day. Each sortie carried its own mental and physical strains.

In the experience of this author, constant operational flying without a break produces a dulling effect, no matter how high the morale; coupled with tiredness, this leads to loss of efficiency and perhaps even a feeling of resignation about the inevitable end. Bomber and Coastal Command crews were usually given a day off to recover after an operational flight, although of course their flights were

Reichsmarschall Hermann Goering visiting airfields near the Channel coast. Left to right: General der Flieger Hans Jeschonnek, Chief of Staff of the Luftwaffe; General der Flieger Bruno Lörzer, Commander of II. Fliegerkorps; Hermann Goering; Hauptmann Berndt von Brauchitsch, Gruppen-Kommandeur of IV. (Stuka)/LG1 and son of Feldmarschall Walther von Brauchitsch, Supreme Commander of the German Armed Forces.

Jean-Louis Roba collection

generally of far longer duration than a single fighter sortie. But the only remission for fighter pilots in the forefront of the Battle of Britain came in periods of bad weather. Dowding recognised these problems and seems to have acted wisely. Nevertheless, his rotation of squadrons meant that about a third of the squadrons in No. 11 Group in this period were relatively inexperienced. In the opinion of some of the veterans, this led to a higher proportion of losses in these squadrons.

There was cloudy weather for the next few days but on 19 August a few bombers reached the outskirts of London while others bombed Pembroke docks. There were scattered raids on targets at night. The Luftflotten lost eleven aircraft, mostly in accidents, with two damaged, while Fighter Command lost five with one damaged but repairable. The following day also saw limited activity in poor weather, but there were some daylight attacks against shipping and airfields in the south-east. The Luftflotten lost eight aircraft and four damaged, while Fighter Command lost only two, plus two damaged but repairable.

On 21 August Goering made his first visit to the forward headquarters of Luftflotte 2 in France, accompanied by his deputy Milch. Kesselring, Sperrle and Lörzer were also present, while Goering peered at the RDF station at Dover through a pair of powerful binoculars. According to Adolf Galland's autobiography, it was on this occasion that he was once more upbraided by Goering for what was regarded as the failure of the fighter arm to give adequate protection to the bombers. Galland was stung and embittered by the harsh and unjustified criticism. He wrote that when Goering simmered down somewhat and asked if there was anything he wanted, he unwisely replied by asking for a squadron of Spitfires, even though he believed that the Bf109 was the better fighter. Apparently Goering growled with rage, turned and stumped off.

Activity during the day on 21 August was mostly confined to small formations making hit-and-run attacks against airfields. In operations and accidents fourteen Luftflotten aircraft were lost on operations and one damaged. Luftflotte 5 took little part in the operations during this phase, but it suffered a steady trickle of losses from reconnaissance sorties or accidents. Fighter Command lost one Spitfire in combat, three Blenheims destroyed on the ground, and eight aircraft damaged but repairable.

The next day brought a series of reconnaissance flights and an attack on a convoy passing Dover, followed by an increase of activity at night. Four German aircraft were lost while four more were damaged, while Fighter Command also lost four aircraft plus eight damaged in combat or accidents but repairable. An attempt was made on this day to improve the air-sea rescue service by placing twelve Lysanders of Army Co-operation Command under the direct control of Fighter Command and dispersing them at airfields around the coast, from where they carried out searches of up to 20 miles distance. Naval patrol boats and RAF launches came under the operational control of the Royal Navy. However, this service remained inadequate until a Directorate of Sea Rescue was set up under Coastal Command in January 1941. With Marshal of the Royal Air Force Sir John Salmond as Director-General of Aircraft and Aircrew Safety, it then made rapid improvements. The number of RAF launches increased rapidly, and Supermarine Walrus amphibians were used for picking up ditched airmen. Later in 1941 RAF squadrons devoted entirely to air-sea rescue were formed.

Bad weather continued to limit operations on 23 August, with scattered attacks in daylight made by single or up to three aircraft. Night attacks were made on much the same scale. The Luftflotten lost eight aircraft during the day, with seven damaged. Fighter Command lost one aircraft in an accident, plus five damaged for a variety of reasons but repairable.

Fine weather on 24 August brought evidence of the change in German tactics determined five days earlier, and these soon gave rise to concern. The new method was to patrol the Straits of Dover with a series of formations at varying heights, with occasional feints towards the English coast. These manoeuvres lasted from dawn to dusk, and were designed to confuse and exhaust the defending RAF squadrons. Many of the fighters in Luftflotte 3 had been transferred to Luftflotte 2, leaving the bombers in the air fleet to concentrate partially on night operations.

A sudden attack on Manston caused considerable damage, although some bombers and fighters were shot down. Another raid on the same station in the afternoon put it completely out of action, with communications cut off. Although telephone engineers worked miracles, Fighter Command abandoned the station temporarily. Other attacks hit the town of Ramsgate in Kent and the airfields of North Weald and Hornchurch in Essex. Portsmouth and Southampton were bombed by Luftflotte 3, escorted by its remaining fighters. Over a hundred people were killed when Portsmouth town and dockyard were hit. During the night the City of London and central London were bombed, although accidentally, as well as some of the suburbs to the east and north-east. Many other towns throughout England were hit by small groups of bombers. The Luftflotten caused widespread damage, but it was not an easy day for them, with forty-one aircraft lost and seven damaged. Fighter Command's casualties were relatively higher than usual, with twenty aircraft lost and eighteen damaged but repairable.

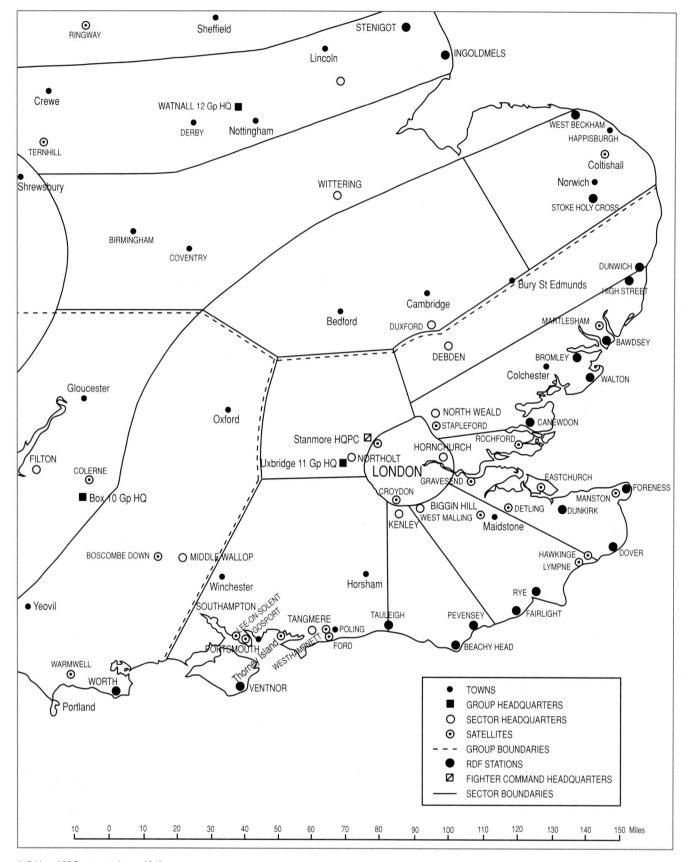

Airfields and RDF stations in August 1940.

Most of the attacks on 25 August were confined to the late afternoon. Feints and small raids took place and a major raid occurred when Luftflotte 3 despatched a formation which headed towards Weymouth in Dorset, where it was tackled by squadrons of No. 10 Group. The fighter airfield at Warmwell was bombed, damaging two hangars. A formation from Luftflotte 2 approached Dover but was intercepted by eleven squadrons of No. 11 Group. The Luftflotten lost twenty-one aircraft in operations and accidents during the day, with ten more damaged. Fighter Command's losses were relatively heavy, with fourteen aircraft lost and five damaged but repairable.

During the night Bomber Command despatched 103 aircraft to targets in Germany and France. About half of them were sent to Berlin, sanctioned by the War Cabinet in retaliation for the bombs dropped on London during the previous night. The crews met strong head-winds and thick cloud covered the German capital. Almost all the bombs fell on farms to the south of the city, and only two people were slightly injured in Berlin itself. Three Hampdens were shot down and three more ditched in the North Sea on the return journey. It was an ineffective attack which resulted in some derision from Berliners, but more serious raids were to follow.

There were three strong attacks by the Luftflotten during the next day, 26 August. Bombs were dropped on the RAF stations at Biggin Hill and Kenley in the late morning, followed by attacks against North Weald, Debden and Hornchurch in the early afternoon. Some factories in Kent and Essex were also hit. Later in the afternoon Luftflotte 3 sent a formation to Portsmouth. All these attacks were met by strong defences. It was a bad day for both sides. The two Luftflotten lost forty-three aircraft in operations and accidents, with fourteen others damaged, while Fighter Command lost twenty-eight aircraft plus nineteen damaged but repairable. This was Luftflotte 3's last major daylight raid for several weeks, its activities being turned over to the night operations decreed by Goering. During the night Plymouth, Coventry and Birmingham were all bombed.

A disagreement between two of the RAF's Group commanders broke out on 26 August, when Park wrote to Dowding complaining that the squadrons sent from No. 12 Group under Air Vice-Marshal Leigh-Mallory, under the rotation system, were of poorer quality than those sent from No. 13 Group under Air Vice-Marshal Saul. He stated that three squadrons sent from Saul had shot down forty-three enemy aircraft at the cost of four of their own, while the two sent from Leigh-Mallory had shot down only seventeen enemy aircraft but lost thirteen of their own number. On the following day Park wrote complaining that No. 12 Group was failing to respond when asked to patrol airfields of No. 11 Group. The reason was that the Group was attempting (unsuccessfully) to form 'Big Wings' in response to the requests, and the squadrons were arriving late after trying to form up. In response Leigh-Mallory stated that the requests were arriving too late for him to take the necessary action. This unhappy disagreement was to intensify in the next few weeks.

Bombs exploding near Folkestone in Kent during a midday raid on 27 August 1940. This was a cloudy and rainy day with somewhat less activity than usual.

Bruce Robertson collection

There were few attacks on 27 August, despite reasonable flying conditions. Enemy activity was mainly confined to reconnaissance, with some night attacks on the Midlands. Nevertheless, the three Luftflotten lost eleven aircraft in combat or accidents, with ten more damaged, while Fighter Command lost seven aircraft, mostly in accidents, plus two damaged but repairable.

The daylight offensive was resumed on the next day, 28 August. It began with a determined attack on the Coastal Command station of Eastchurch in Kent and the Fighter Command base of Rochford in Essex. Many of the bombers broke through in spite of interception. The Defiants of 264 Squadron had been brought down to Rochford from Kirton-in-Lindsey in Lincolnshire six days before and were unwisely sent up, presumably to avoid being destroyed on the ground. The result was inevitable. Three were shot down, with five crew members killed, and three more returned severely damaged but repairable. The remainder of the squadron was sent back to Kirton-in-Lindsey later in the day and employed on the far more suitable role of night-fighting.

Sweeps by Messerschmitt Bf109s also took place on this day, at 25,000ft over Kent. In spite of Park's instruction that fighter versus fighter combat should be avoided, seven squadrons were sent up to intercept them, and equal numbers on both sides were shot down. At night Liverpool and Birkenhead received the first of four heavy raids, on the instructions of Goering. Manchester, Birmingham, Coventry, Sheffield, Derby and London also received quotas of bombs. The Luftflotten lost thirty-one aircraft during the day, with thirteen damaged. One of these was an aircraft rarely seen by the RAF, a Gotha Go145-B biplane of Stab Jagdgeschwader 27 which had been delivering mail to the German-occupied Channel Islands. The pilot lost his way and landed on Lewes racecourse in Sussex, where he was taken prisoner. Including the Defiants, Fighter Command lost sixteen aircraft plus eight damaged but repairable.

Luftflotte 2 resumed daylight attacks on targets in the south-east during the morning of the next day, 30 August. The formations were able to fly above a layer of cloud at 7,000ft, reducing the effectiveness of the Observer Corps. Park requested reinforcements from No. 12 Group but the attackers slipped through and caused damage at Biggin Hill. In the afternoon Coastal Command's station at Detling in Kent was put out of action for the day and the civil airport at Luton in Bedfordshire was also bombed. But the most effective attack was another against Biggin Hill. The raiders blew up hangars and workshops, severed all power, and killed or wounded sixty-five personnel. The ground services of this station suffered the worst of any organisation within Fighter Command. The day cost the Luftflotten forty aircraft lost and eleven damaged. It was not a good day for Fighter Command, which lost twenty-five aircraft in combat and one destroyed on the ground, plus fifteen damaged but repairable. Fortunately, fifteen pilots were saved.

On 31 August Park took additional measures to protect his airfields but waves of German bombers continued to break through on both sides of the Thames. Biggin Hill, Debden and Hornchurch were badly damaged once more, while Duxford, North Weald and Croydon were less seriously hit. Park was forced to withdraw two of his three squadrons at Biggin Hill and place them elsewhere for more than a week while repairs were undertaken. Other attacks were made on RDF stations in Kent and Sussex, with little damage. The night brought more heavy attacks against Birkenhead and Liverpool, with scattered attacks against other cities and towns. The Luftflotten lost thirty-nine aircraft with twenty-five damaged. Fighter Command also lost thirty-nine aircraft, with two more destroyed on the ground, plus fourteen damaged but repairable. With losses of aircraft and pilots reaching parity, the situation for the defences was becoming very serious indeed.

This photograph of a Heinkel He111 was taken by Kriegsberichter (war reporter) Wanderer during a daylight bombing raid over London. It appeared in a 1940 issue of the German magazine *Der Adler* with the caption 'Here they release their high-explosive bombs, hitting the docks, harbour works and railways at the port of Tilbury on the north shore of the Thames.' However, the photograph was evidently taken on 15 August 1940 near North Seaton in Northumberland.

J. Falconer collection

September opened with a continuation of the attacks on airfields, in the fine weather of the late summer. Luftflotte 2 sent over a large formation in mid-morning which split up to deliver attacks on the airfields at Eastchurch, Biggin Hill and Detling, and Tilbury Docks. Another formation in the early afternoon attacked the same targets. Two more formations in the later afternoon attacked Hawkinge, Lympne, Detling and Biggin Hill. At the latter, the operations room which controlled the whole sector was destroyed. The night brought yet another attack on Birkenhead, as well as on other centres. The Luftflotten lost sixteen aircraft and eleven damaged, while Fighter Command lost thirteen aircraft plus eleven damaged but repairable. With these losses still running roughly at parity and the crews on both sides suffering from exhaustion and stress, it was becoming a question of which side could hold out longer.

The next day, 2 September, was a continuation of the same remorseless programme. Luftflotte 2 despatched an even greater number of aircraft during the day, the first formation attacking Eastchurch, Biggin Hill, Rochford and North Weald in the early morning. This was followed by raids east of London in the early afternoon and more bombs on Biggin Hill, Eastchurch, Kenley and Hornchurch three hours later. The last attacks in daylight took place against the same airfields at about 17.30 hours. The usual scattered raids took place at night. The Luftflotten lost thirty-seven aircraft and seventeen damaged. The odds now swung in favour of Fighter Command, with fifteen aircraft written off and seventeen damaged but repairable. Of course, the number of aircrew lost by the Luftflotten usually exceeded those of Fighter Command, partly since most of the actions were fought over English territory.

The mauling continued on 3 September, with the first formations heading for airfields in Essex. The operations room at North Weald received a direct hit but was

THE HAMPSHIRE SPITFIRE SONG

Words and Music
by
H. M. KING.

Price: SIXPENCE.

All profits on the sale of this song are for the "Hampshire Spitfire Fund. - - - -

Dedicated to all British Airmen—especially Frank.

Cover drawn by Master G. MEW.

J. Falconer collection

HAMPSHIRE SPITFIRE FUND

AIM : To buy a **SPITFIRE** or **SPITFIRES** to give to the Nation in honour of our brave airmen.

¶ Towns and villages are asked to set up Committees or appeal for Funds in other ways.

¶ Large towns are raising a Spitfire on their own—but every bit of Hampshire can take part in this glorious piece of war service and raise funds for one of the Hampshire Spitfires.

¶ Is there a Spitfire Committee in your town or village ? If not, find other patriots and get to to work at once. We want every spot in Hampshire to take part in the great campaign.

¶ Collecting-sheets, posters and further details may be obtained from :

Hon. Organiser—Dr. H. M. KING,
109 Holdenhurst Road,
Bournemouth.

¶ Gifts may be made to your local Committee or direct to the Hon. Organiser.

¶ **HELP US TO PUT OUR HAMPSHIRE SPITFIRES IN THE SKY!**

(The music was drawn by H. L. ARCHER).

J. Falconer collection

During a raid against Hornchurch airfield on 31 August 1940, Hurricane Is of 310 (Czech) Squadron from Duxford damaged this Dornier Do17Z-2, coded 5K+LM, of II./Kampfgeschwader 3 from Deurne airfield near Antwerp. The pilot tried to escape by flying low but was hit by anti-aircraft fire and force-landed on the beach at Pegwell Bay, near Ramsgate. All four crew members were wounded and captured.

Philip Jarrett collection

not put completely out of action. The bombers missed other targets. A later attack in the same area was broken up by the defenders. Attacks during the day were beaten off in fierce air battles. The night was quieter than usual, with only a series of single aircraft making nuisance raids. It was a costly day for the Luftflotten, with thirty-three aircraft lost and eight damaged, while Fighter Command lost nineteen aircraft in operations or accidents, plus twelve damaged but repairable.

By the end of this phase, the situation had begun to look critical for No. 11 Group. Four of the seven sector airfields had been so badly damaged that they were becoming unusable by the squadrons normally based on them. These were

Hornchurch, North Weald, Biggin Hill and Kenley. Other airfields in the Group were in much the same condition. It seemed possible that the squadrons might have to be withdrawn to more distant airfields, leaving London and the southeast of England partly unprotected and more vulnerable to a seaborne and airborne invasion. But this did not happen, for Hitler and Goering instituted another change of policy. Park wrote soon afterwards: 'Had the enemy continued his heavy attacks against Biggin Hill and adjacent sectors, and knocked out their operations rooms or telephone communications, the fighter defences of London would have been in a parlous state during the last critical phase. . . .'

A Junkers Ju88A-1 of Kampfgeschwader 77 at Loon-Plage, near Dunkirk, in September 1940. The purpose of the light-coloured bar on the fin was to provide quick identification in the air.

Dornier Do17Z-2, F1+AL, of the 3rd Staffel, I./Kampfgeschwader 76, at Beauvais airfield in France during the Battle of Britain. The lettering on the entrance hatch reads 'ZURÜCK. Um dem Motor herumgehen. Von hinten einsteigen' (GET BACK. Go round the engines. Enter from behind).

One of the Wellington Is which raided Berlin on the night of 25/26 August 1940, being serviced on its return. Bomber Command despatched 81 aircraft to the German capital on that night, in retaliation for some bombs which had fallen on London. Very little damage was caused but it was the first of several such attacks which infuriated Hitler and caused the Luftwaffe to abandon attacks against RAF airfields and switch to bombing London.

Author's collection

A British lance corporal pointing to the insignia
of a Junkers 88, possibly of 7./Kampfgeschwader
4, brought down in the Battle of Britain.

Philip Jarrett collection

Leutnant Krug under guard on the quayside
after being brought in by the Margate lifeboat on
28 August 1940. His Dornier Do17Z-3 coded
5K+LP of 6./Kampfgeschwader 3 ditched in the
sea off Foreness Point when damaged in combat
with RAF fighters. The other three crew
members were also rescued.

Bruce Robertson collection

Groundcrews of Kampfgeschwader 55 handling an armour-piercing bomb in front of one of their Heinkel 111s in France during the Battle of Britain.

(*Overleaf*) 'SQUADRON LEADER DOUGLAS
BADER'S HURRICANE'
by Charles J. Thompson
Hurricane I serial V7487 of 242 Squadron
coming in to land at Duxford in Cambridgeshire
in 1940.

RAF Hemswell in Lincolnshire received a
surprise visitor in the evening of 29 August 1940
when an unidentified German aircraft (probably
a Messerschmitt Bf110) made a diving attack
and dropped a 250kg bomb on the edge of the
parade ground. The bomb did not explode and
the station armaments officer examined it, at
considerable risk to himself. After taking
precautions, he deliberately exploded it, as
shown here. No injuries were caused to
personnel and there was no damage to
buildings.

Author's collection

On 24 August 1940 Messerschmitt Bf109E-4 of
6./Jagdgeschwader 51 'Mölders' was damaged in
combat with a Hurricane I of 56 Squadron based
at North Weald in Essex. The pilot,
Oberfeldwebel Fritz Beeck, force-landed in a
field near East Langdon in Kent and was
captured uninjured. The unit emblem on the
fuselage showed a weeping pelican with the
motto 'Gott Strafe England'.

Philip Jarrett collection

The smoking remains of a yellow-nosed Messerschmitt Bf109 shot down at West Wickham in Kent during a daylight attack on London.

Author's collection

A Messerschmitt Bf109E-4B of an unknown unit, carrying an SC 250kg bomb attached to its ETC500 bomb rack.

Georges Van Acker collection

This MG15 7.92mm calibre gun was taken from
the dorsal position of a Heinkel He111 brought
down in Kent and remounted in a position held
by a company of the Somerset Light Infantry.
Within a few minutes of its installation, this
gunner was credited with bringing down a
Messerschmitt Bf109.

Author's collection

Dornier Do17Z-3 coded 5K+ER of
7./Kampfgeschwader 3 force-landed in the sea
off Foreness Point on the Isle of Thanet during
the early afternoon of 26 August 1940. It was
damaged by a Hurricane when attempting to
bomb West Malling airfield. Two of the crew
drowned, one died later from wounds and the
other became a prisoner. This photograph was
taken at low tide.

Philip Jarrett collection

Output of repaired Hurricane Is at Cowley in Oxfordshire. This was the home of No. 1 Civilian Repair Unit and the RAF's No. 50 Maintenance Unit. Control was split between a civilian superintendent from Morris Motors Ltd and an RAF officer from No. 43 Group.

Bruce Robertson collection

(*Right*) The airman second from the left appears to be receiving a reprimand from the Staffelkäpitan in this photograph. Heinkel He111H-2 is at dispersal in the background.

Jean-Louis Roba collection

(*Previous page*) 'CHANNEL CROSSING' by Charles J. Thompson
A Heinkel He111H-1 of II./Kampfgeschwader 53 in the foreground and a Heinkel He111H-3 of 6./Kampfgeschwader 55 in the background, over the English Channel in September 1940.

Air raid warden Miss Sonia Vera Carlyle was awarded a George Medal for her actions on 1 September 1940. Without assistance, she attended a number of badly injured women and children in bombed houses in Caterham, Surrey, and treated others for shock. She was 19 years of age.

Author's collection

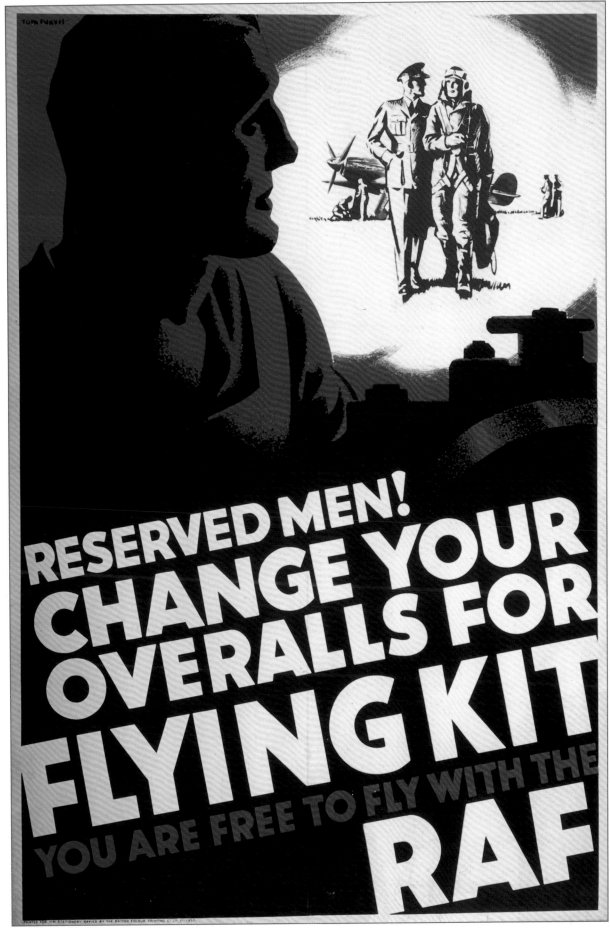

Royal Air Force Museum FA10774

This Heinkel He111H-2 coded V4+HV of
Kampfgeschwader I was shot down on
30 August 1940 by a Hurricane of
253 Squadron from Kenley, during an attack on
Farnborough airfield. It force-landed at Haxted
Farm, near Lingfield in Surrey. One crew
member was killed and the other four crew
members were captured, two of them wounded.
Philip Jarrett collection

CHAPTER SEVEN

BLITZ BY DAY AND NIGHT

In early September 1940 the Wehrmacht's plans for the invasion of Britain were complete. Most of the troops detailed for the first echelons had reached their assembly points and the remainder did so by the middle of the month. By 4 September there were 168 transports waiting to carry the assault forces over the Channel, but the Kriegsmarine needed notice before sweeping the British minefields and laying its own. It was expected that Hitler would give the order to commence operations by 11 September, so that the landings would commence ten days later. The initial echelons would be followed by larger waves, as related in Chapter Three. Meanwhile Hitler studied reports from the Luftwaffe, waiting a satisfactory outcome of the air war before giving his orders.

In the intervening weeks since Dunkirk, the British anti-invasion measures had improved considerably. More than 400 25lb field guns had been added to those already in service. The armoured units had been equipped with about 250 medium or cruiser tanks, while there were over 500 light tanks armed with machine-guns. There were four light anti-aircraft batteries ready to deal with dive-bombers. The infantry divisions numbered twenty-seven, but about half had not completed their training and only twelve were well equipped. The Home Guard numbered about half a million men and could be expected to support the divisions in the defence of local areas. The coastal defences and minefields inland or out to sea had been extended and could constitute a severe hindrance to the enemy. The assembly of barges and landing craft at ports in France and the Low Countries was known from photo-reconnaissance, and these received due attention from Bomber Command. But there was no knowledge of the probable date for an invasion. The troops stood to at dawn every day while their commanders were under orders to move immediately to battle stations when the code-word 'Cromwell' was given.

The Luftwaffe had made preparations to support the intended landings. The Junkers Ju87 dive-bomber units were concentrated under Luftflotte 2 and stationed opposite the Straits of Dover. Two bomber Geschwaders of Luftflotte 5 had been moved from bases in Scandinavia to reinforce Luftflotte 2. On 7 September almost 600 bombers or dive-bombers together with about 700 fighters were under the command of Feldmarschall Albert Kesselring, while Feldmarschall Hugo Sperrle in command of Luftflotte 2 further west still had at his disposal about 350 bombers and 100 fighters. Yet the war of attrition against Fighter Command had not been won.

In the previous fortnight something had happened in Germany to cause a change of tactics. Bomber Command had been intensifying its nightly bombing operations against the German heartland as well as making attacks on ports and airfields. Then Berlin was bombed on the nights of 3/4 and 4/5 September. Although the damage was not considerable, these raids had begun to cause considerable resentment with the public. They were an embarrassment to Goering who on 9 August 1939 had declared to a group of businessmen: 'If an enemy bomber reaches the Ruhr, my name is not Hermann Goering; you can call me Meyer!'

Hitler was also convinced that his country was invulnerable from the air. Before the war, his architect Albert Speer had been ordered to draw up plans for an enormous government complex in Berlin, 825ft in diameter with a dome rising to 726ft and a central turret rising another 132ft, then topped by a German eagle and a swastika. It would have been at least 900ft high and Speer was warned that it would be visible above low cloud and could act as an aiming point for enemy bombers. When he relayed this to Hitler, the reply was: 'Goering has assured me that no enemy plane will fly over Germany. We will not let that sort of thing stand in the way of our plans.' But now the RAF was over Berlin, although the crews did not have the benefit of this monstrous edifice, for it was never built. Goering's words were to cause much bitterness among the German people in the coming months and years.

Plans for retaliation against London were drawn up and authorised by Hitler, as a prelude to the invasion itself. It was believed that the daylight part of a round-the-clock attack against the capital would bring the remnants of Fighter Command to battle and result in their destruction. Hitler made a speech in Berlin on 4 September, in which he derided the British and included the comment: 'In England they are filled with curiosity and keep asking "Why doesn't he come?" Keep calm. He is coming! He is coming! . . . When they declare they will increase their attacks on our cities, then we will raze their cities to the ground.'

Hermann Goering on board his personal train *Asien* (Asia) with members of his staff. On his left is Hans Jeschonnek, the Chief of Staff of the Luftwaffe, who committed suicide on 19 August 1943.

Jean-Louis Roba collection

Goering decided to be present when the assault began on 7 September. His private train steamed down to the Pas de Calais, where the commanders of the Luftflotten were gathered with their staffs. The day began with a series of small attacks against airfields in the south east, of the routine type expected by Fighter Command. The British knew the 'Order of Battle' of the various Luftflotten, from decryption of enemy signals, but not the exact strength of the various units nor the intentions of the German High Command. The attack against London was not anticipated and the squadrons were still deployed in defence of their airfields. The main enemy force arrived at about 17.00 hours, consisting of about 300 bombers escorted by twice that number of Bf109s and Bf110s, all from Luftflotte 2. The RAF controllers expected this huge fleet to break up into

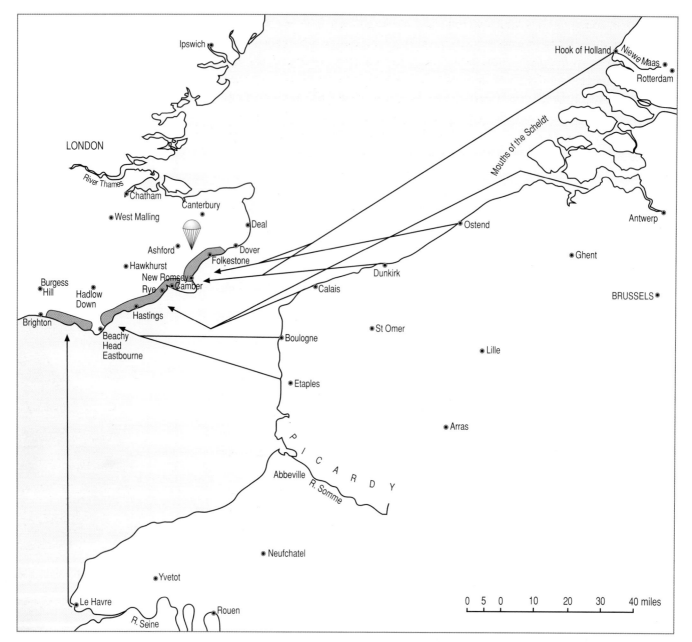

The German plan for invasion by sea and air in
September 1940.

smaller formations, but this did not happen. All the bombers headed for the
docks and oil installations in the lower reaches of the Thames where they
encountered anti-aircraft defences depleted by withdrawal to other threatened
areas. For the most part, the attackers were not tackled by Fighter Command
until after the bombs and incendiaries had been dropped. Many fires were caused
and these could not be extinguished before nightfall.

Other formations approached the south-east coast and also headed for London,
this time to be tackled by the defending fighters before and after reaching their
objective. For some reason, the code-word 'Cromwell' was given in some areas,
church bells were rung, and the Home Guard was alerted.

A stream of about 250 bombers from Luftflotte 3 arrived over London during
the night, from about 20.30 hours until dawn, with the fires left by the earlier
formations acting as beacons for the crews. These dropped a combination of
high-explosives and incendiaries, mostly on the East End. More fires were started
and these joined up to form huge conflagrations. Others areas of London were

also hit and some power stations were forced to close down. The attackers met little opposition from the defences, apart from the balloon barrage which prevented them from flying at low level and an inadequate anti-aircraft barrage. The Blenheim IFs of Fighter Command did their best to intercept, but their airborne interception RDF was rudimentary and they had little success. There was heavy damage in the docks area and also in thickly populated residential streets. More than 400 Londoners were killed and 1,600 severely injured. Goering boasted in a broadcast, 'This is the historic hour when our air force for the first time delivered its stroke right into the enemy's heart.'

The day cost the Germans forty-one aircraft written off from all causes, with seventeen damaged, while Fighter Command lost seventeen aircraft plus twenty-one damaged but repairable. It was the beginning of the Blitz, which would last until the following May. But these terrible events meant a respite for Fighter Command's battered airfields. However, Dowding felt he could no longer deny Park's request for experienced pilots to be transferred to No. 11 Group from other groups. On the following day, he put into force a 'Stabilisation Scheme' whereby pilots with known ability were drafted into Park's squadrons, while those squadrons further afield had to make do with replacements from the training schools.

The next day, 8 September, brought bad weather and a decrease in enemy activity. Some attacks took place against airfields in Kent during the late morning, but Londoners suffered another raid at night, killing over 400 more civilians and injuring about 750. Fifteen German aircraft were lost and eight damaged, while Fighter Command lost five aircraft and three damaged but repairable.

On 9 September the enemy formations arrived in the afternoon, but Fighter Command had anticipated these attacks and made its dispositions accordingly. Most of the formations were broken up and the bombs dropped haphazardly, with the Luftwaffe crews surprised at the strength of the resistance. But almost 200 bombers came over London in relays during the night and all districts suffered, with 370 people killed and 1,400 injured. The Luftflotten lost thirty aircraft plus fifteen damaged, while eighteen aircraft of Fighter Command were written off plus fourteen damaged but repairable.

The German High Commanders were puzzled at the continued strength of a Fighter Command which by their calculations had been almost wiped out. They did not seem to appreciate that the Luftwaffe's claims of enemy aircraft destroyed were three or four times greater than the true losses. RAF fighters were coming up against their formations with no apparent decline in numbers.

Hitler postponed his decision about the date of the invasion, originally intended to be issued to the Wehrmacht on 11 September, for three more days. He expected to announce on this day a revised date of 24 September for the commencement of Operation Sealion, but meanwhile hoped that the heavy bombing of London would result in a repeat performance of the bombing of Warsaw and Rotterdam, which had forced the surrender of Poland and the Netherlands. He expected so much panic among British civilians that the Government would face collapse and at last seek terms with the Third Reich.

Once more, though, he had gravely underestimated the fortitude of the British people. If anything, the bombing had stiffened their resolve, for their main cry was for retaliation against Berlin by Bomber Command. In truth, the German people faced an appalling future. Hitler and Goering were 'sowing the wind' and the citizens of their country would 'reap the whirlwind'.

The morning and afternoon of 10 September were fairly uneventful but about a hundred bombers raided London at night while others ranged further afield to South Wales and Merseyside. Civilian casualties in London were reported as 19 killed and 290 injured. The Luftflotten lost only five aircraft during the day, with five more damaged, but eight Heinkel He111s were destroyed on the ground during an attack by Bomber Command on Eindhoven airfield while two more were damaged. Three aircraft of Fighter Command were written off and three more were damaged but repairable.

In the afternoon of 11 September formations from Luftflotte 2 headed once more for London while others from Luftflotte 3 attacked Portsmouth and Southampton. Attempts were also made to jam the RDF system, causing some interference. By then, Park had realised that the Luftflotten had changed their tactics to mass raids, with waves arriving over the same target in quick succession. He ordered his squadrons to attack in a series of pairs, Spitfires against Bf109s and Hurricanes against the bombers and their close escorts. London received another heavy night attack, but the anti-aircraft barrage had been reinforced and the great thunder of the guns gave some satisfaction to civilians. There was less damage, but casualties were reported as 110 killed and 260 seriously injured. The Luftflotten lost twenty-nine aircraft plus nineteen damaged. Fighter Command's losses were heavy, with twenty-seven aircraft written off and twenty damaged but repairable.

Cloud and rain put a stop to most of the daylight activities on 12 September, and night bombing was correspondingly reduced. Some bombers flew over London and other targets scattered around England and Wales. Casualties in London were given as fifty-seven killed and eighty-four seriously injured. However, the Luftflotten lost seven aircraft plus seven damaged, while Fighter Command lost only one, on a non-operational flight. The bad weather persisted on 13 September, with only small raids in daylight over Kent and Sussex, and about a hundred bombers over London at night. Casualties in London and elsewhere were reported as 37 killed and 270 injured. The Germans lost six aircraft, one of which collided with a balloon cable at Ellesmere Port in South Wales, and two damaged. Another aircraft was written off after an attack by the RAF on Boulogne. Fighter Command lost three aircraft plus one damaged but repairable. The next day, 14 September, was at first cloudy and rainy but three formations from Luftflotte 2 headed for London in the afternoon and there were clashes with Fighter Command. The night brought more attacks against London and other cities, resulting in about 100 civilians killed and over 400 injured. German losses amounted to thirteen aircraft written off and eight damaged. Fighter Command lost twelve aircraft, plus eleven damaged but repairable. The German crews felt that opposition was weakening and that the RAF could be nearing collapse. Hitler and Goering hoped that one more major effort would bring the desired results.

The weather on 15 September was fine, after a misty start. Mass formations from Luftflotte 2 arrived over Britain shortly before midday, at altitudes of 15,000ft and above, and were tackled by all three RAF Groups. Twenty-four Hurricane and Spitfire squadrons were put into the air and made a succession of attacks before the bombers reached London. Leigh-Mallory at last managed to form one of his 'Big Wings', consisting of three squadrons of Hurricanes and two of Spitfires. The enemy formations broke up and most of the bombs missed their intended targets, falling over widely dispersed districts of the capital.

Another formation, in three waves, arrived over England at about 14.00 hours, but during the lull the RAF fighters had been rearmed and were waiting. Once

A stick of six bombs exploded in the grounds of Buckingham Palace on 13 September 1940. The King and Queen were showered with glass in a nearby room. The Palace had been slightly damaged in an attack three days earlier. The King and Queen are seen here chatting to air raid precaution staff who were dealing with the wreckage. The Queen was reported as saying 'Now we can look the East End in the face.'

Author's collection

again, Leigh-Mallory contributed a five-squadron wing. The German formation was harried on the way to London and on its return, dropping its bombs haphazardly. Luftflotte 3 sent a smaller formation over Portland but the anti-aircraft barrage seems to have confused the bombing, which was inaccurate. One squadron from No. 10 Group tore into the attackers on their return journey. Yet another formation, of twin-engined Bf110s, tried to bomb the Supermarine Works near Southampton at about 18.00 hours and was also pursued and attacked when over the sea. Night bombing took place on London, as usual, while smaller attacks were made on Cardiff, Bristol, Liverpool and Manchester. Civilian casualties were reported as 62 killed and 119 seriously injured.

This was the day when 185 aircraft were claimed as destroyed by the RAF, a record that was received with jubilation by the public. In fact the Luftflotten lost fifty-nine aircraft during the day, with twenty-two others damaged. Fighter Command wrote off fourteen aircraft, while eleven others were damaged but repairable. Six single-engined pilots lost their lives as well as the two-man crew of a Beaufighter. One Spitfire pilot ditched near the French coast and was taken prisoner. It was a clear victory for the RAF and the day is rightly considered to have been the climax of the campaign. It is celebrated annually as 'Battle of Britain Day'.

The momentous events of 15 September were followed by a day of cloud and rain, resulting in little daylight activity. Goering called his Luftflotten

This Dornier Do17Z, F1+FH, of Kampfgeschwader 76 took off from Beauvais in France at 10.05 hours on 15 September 1940 as part of an attack on central London. It lagged behind the formation owing to engine trouble and was attacked by Hurricanes of 310 (Czech) and 504 Squadrons and then by Spitfires of 609 Squadron. The wireless operator and flight mechanic baled out and were captured but the air observer and rear gunner were killed. The pilot, Oberleutnant Robert Zehbe, also baled out and came down in Kennington, where he was assaulted by civilians and died of his injuries. The aircraft broke up and part of the remains fell on the corner of Victoria station and Wilton Road, as shown here.

Author's collection

Messerschmitt Bf109E-7 of 3. (J)/Lehr-
geschwader 2 Staffel was shot down on
15 September 1940 and crash-landed at
Shellness Point in the Isle of Sheppey. The pilot,
Unteroffizier August Click, was captured unhurt.
Someone has chalked U/S (unserviceable) on
the fuselage.

Philip Jarrett collection

(Previous page) 'DUXFORD SCRAMBLE'
by Mark Postlethwaite
Hurricane Is taking off from Duxford in
Cambridgeshire to form a 'Big Wing', with
aircraft of 242 (Canadian) Squadron in the
foreground and those of 310 (Czechoslovakian)
Squadron in the background.

commanders and their senior officers to a conference in which he ordered a
return to attacks designed to wipe out Fighter Command. The mass formations
sent to bomb London should be split into smaller units unless the weather was
particularly favourable, and the raids against aircraft factories should be
intensified. Although recognising that his pilots and their crews were becoming
tired, Goering thought – once again – that another four or five days of conflict
would be sufficient to destroy the enemy. As obtuse as ever, he still stuck to his
belief that Britain could be brought to its knees by the might of the Luftwaffe
alone and that an invasion would not be necessary.

Park also issued an instruction, criticizing the failure of some squadrons to
rendezvous in time, delays by controllers in vectoring aircraft on to the enemy,
and too many attacks being made on high-flying fighters instead of the bombers.
There were only minor attacks during the day but heavy raids on London
resumed at night, together with smaller raids on Bristol and Liverpool. Civilian
casualties during the day in all areas amounted about 75 killed and 420 injured.
The Luftflotten lost twelve aircraft from all causes, with seven more damaged,
while Fighter Command lost only one aircraft, with three more damaged but
repairable.

The next day, 17 September, brought squally weather and thunderstorms.
Waves of fighters, escorting a few bombers, attempted to lure Hurricane and
Spitfire squadrons into combat, and some encounters took place. Night raids
were at full strength, mainly over London but with some diversions as far as
Merseyside and Glasgow. Oxford Street in London was especially badly hit.
Civilian casualties in all areas were reported as about 175 killed and 575 injured.

The Luftflotten lost eight aircraft, with nine more damaged, while Fighter Command lost six, with eight more damaged but repairable.

Hitler ordered the indefinite postponement of Operation Sealion on this day. Although he gave the uncertain weather as the main reason, the failure of the Luftwaffe to destroy Fighter Command must have been prominent in his thinking, as well as the severe losses his forces were suffering. British Intelligence did not know about this order but an identical signal transmitted on every German naval frequency on 15 September had been noted. This was a very unusual occurrence and it was correctly deduced that this message was associated with a postponement of the invasion. The state of readiness for the anti-invasion forces was relaxed. However, the German commanders still expected Hitler to give the order, perhaps as late as October, and their assault forces remained on a high state of readiness. Meanwhile Bomber Command continued attacks against the Channel ports at night, making major efforts with over a hundred aircraft on each of the nights of 15/16 and 17/18 September.

Better weather on 18 September did not induce Hitler to revoke his decision to postpone the invasion. However, a large formation of fighters tried to penetrate Kent in the early morning but turned back after seventeen RAF squadrons appeared on the scene. Other attempts continued during the morning, some of the bombers reaching London. Fighting was intense and most of the formations were broken up by Nos 11 and 12 Groups. London received its nightly quota of raids, causing much damage in the West End, and Liverpool was also a target. Civilian casualties in all areas were reported as about 240 killed and over 550 injured. The Luftflotten lost twenty aircraft in operations and accidents, with seven more damaged. Fighter Command also lost twenty, with thirteen damaged but repairable. Pilots killed or injured continued to be Dowding's main worry, but the Air Ministry agreed to transfer more of the pilots from the Battle squadrons of Bomber Command, which in any event were converting on to Blenheims, and to allocate to Fighter Command a higher proportion of the pilots coming through the training schools.

On 19 September there were intrusions by single aircraft only during daylight hours, followed by rain at night which restricted operational flying. Civilian casualties in all areas were lighter, with seventeen killed and under a hundred injured. The day cost the Luftflotten ten aircraft, with nine more damaged, while Fighter Command had only one Hurricane slightly damaged after engine failure. Meanwhile the Channel ports were receiving regular visits from Bomber Command and a number of barges and other vessels were sunk. Hitler ordered any further assembly to be stopped and for the ships to be dispersed, to avoid such losses.

During this night an oil bomb fell on Heston airfield, where the Photographic Reconnaissance Unit was based, damaging a number of aircraft including the Lockheed 12A which was the unit's original aircraft. This historic machine was shipped for repair to the USA where, after more recent restoration, it still exists in flying condition. The Photographic Reconnaissance Unit moved to a new base at Benson in Oxfordshire on 27 December, where there was less danger from bombing.

The weather improved on 20 September but enemy activity was still limited to reconnaissance and single intruders during the morning. Some raids against airfields followed in the afternoon and night bombing was restricted. However, civilian casualties in London were reported as 70 killed and 250 injured. German losses were eight aircraft written off and six damaged, while Fighter Command

An accumulation of invasion barges at Dunkirk photographed on 19 September 1940 from a Blenheim IV of 82 Squadron based at Watton in Norfolk. Photo-interpreters were able to detect that some barges had been sunk or damaged by RAF bombing, while cranes and haulage gear had been smashed. Some dock buildings and warehouses had been gutted. Approach roads and railway sidings were pitted with bomb craters. Nevertheless, many barges remained undamaged.

Author's collection

also lost eight aircraft plus four damaged but repairable. Fine weather continued during the next day, when airfields in the south-east were attacked in the early evening, followed by some night raids against London and other cities. Eleven aircraft were written off by the Luftflotten, with three more damaged, while Fighter Command lost one aircraft and two damaged but repairable.

There was an unexpected lull in daylight during 22 September, but a stream of raiders came over London and other cities during the night, resulting in about 45 civilian deaths plus 350 injured. Losses of aircraft on both sides were light, with only six German aircraft written off and five damaged, while Fighter Command lost three, with three more damaged but repairable. Fine weather on the next day brought a series of fighter sweeps over Kent in the direction of London, resulting in air battles, followed by a heavy night raid on London and a smaller attack on

Merseyside. Reported civilian casualties were over 100 killed and 350 injured. The Luftflotten lost seventeen aircraft and four damaged, while Fighter Command lost eleven, plus one damaged but repairable.

During the night of 23/24 September Bomber Command devoted its entire effort to a single city for the first time. The target was Berlin, in retaliation for the attacks on London, with the crews given instructions to hit railway yards, electrical power stations, gasworks and aircraft component factories. Of 129 aircraft which set off, all but ten bombed. Three aircraft were lost. The German records of the results were never disclosed, and it seems probable they were too serious for public consumption. It was not possible to achieve pinpoint accuracy, especially when bombing targets from high level, with the equipment available to the RAF at the time.

There were fairly favourable flying conditions on 24 September, and an enemy formation headed for the East End of London in the morning, followed by an attack by Bf109 fighter-bombers on the Supermarine Works near Southampton during the afternoon. London and Merseyside were attacked at night, resulting in about 110 people killed and about 550 injured. Eleven German aircraft were lost and twelve damaged, while Fighter Command lost six, plus eight damaged but repairable.

These fine weather conditions continued on 25 September, when three Gruppen of Luftflotte 3 made an unexpected attack shortly before midday on the Bristol Aeroplane Company's factory at Filton, near Bristol. Bombs dropped by Heinkel He111s caused much damage, killing about 60 workers, injuring about 150 more and reducing production for several weeks. The controllers in No. 10 Group believed at first that this formation had been making for the Westland factory at Yeovil. The defending fighters were incorrectly vectored, so that only a few eventually caught up with the attackers on their return journey. The night brought more attacks on London, plus some scattered raids elsewhere. Civilian casualties in London amounted about 70 killed and 370 injured. Sixteen aircraft of the Luftflotten were lost during the day, with six more damaged. Fighter Command wrote off seven aircraft, with nine more damaged but repairable.

On 26 September a determined attack was made by Luftflotte 3 on the Supermarine Works at Woolston, near Southampton. The formation arrived in the afternoon and the bombs were dropped accurately, wrecking the factory and causing about a hundred casualties. Production was suspended while repairs took place, and it was the end of the year before full output was achieved. London was raided at night and the Houses of Parliament were hit. German losses were nine aircraft destroyed, with six more damaged, while Fighter Command also lost nine, plus nine damaged but repairable.

In the early morning of 27 September Luftflotte 2 made renewed attempts to bomb London in daylight. These began with Messerschmitt Bf110s carrying bombs and escorted by Bf109s, but the formations were broken up by Spitfires and Hurricanes. Dornier Do17s and Junkers Ju88s followed, apparently having missed their fighter escort, and these were badly mauled by the defenders. Luftflotte 3 then took up the attack, sending a formation later in the morning which split into two, a larger section heading for London and another for Bristol. Both were intercepted and suffered accordingly. Raids at night took place against London, Merseyside and various targets in the Midlands. Civilian casualties in all areas amounted to about 200 killed and 400 injured. It was a very bad day for the Luftflotten, which lost fifty-seven aircraft with another twelve damaged. The intense fighting cost Fighter Command twenty-eight aircraft written off and

Heinkel He111H-3 unit code 1H+GP of
6./Kampfgeschwader 26 'Löwen' was flown by
Unteroffizier Niemeyer on 23/24 September
1940 during a night attack on London. It was
shot down by anti-aircraft fire and crashed near
Gordon Boys Home at Chobham in Surrey and
burnt out. The crew baled out and were
captured.

Author's collection

thirty-two damaged but repairable. Nevertheless, the day was another clear victory for the RAF.

On this day the author was one of several trainees at RAF Prestwick who were given a short leave. He headed for the family home at Woodford Green in Essex, armed with a railway travel warrant but worried about the continued bombing of the London area. A great orange glow could be seen in the night sky miles from King's Cross station, interspersed with bright flashes. The train stopped and started on many occasions, but at last drew into the terminal. Most of the passengers took shelter, but the author found a solitary taxi with a Cockney driver who agreed to try to reach Liverpool Street station. All went well until near Ludgate Circus when the intrepid driver was stopped by blazing buildings and hosepipes over the roads. There was no option but to pay him off and cut through the side streets, using a kitbag as protection from shell splinters and ignoring shouts to take cover. Amazingly, there was a steam train in Liverpool Street station which chugged north-east to Essex, passing between fires in the inner suburbs. The author's family, parents and twin brothers, were safely ensconced in the purpose-built air raid shelter in the garden, fitted with bunk beds. The dog enjoyed these occasions, diving down the ventilation shaft when the sirens sounded.

The Luftflotten fared better on 28 September, when a series of smaller formations came over during daylight and headed for central London. Thirteen aircraft of Fighter Command were shot down and seven more were damaged, whereas the German losses were twelve aircraft written off and only one damaged. London received its nightly quota of bombs, with 70 civilians killed and about 160 injured. These smaller attacks continued during the next day.

Heinkel He111H radio code G1+BH works number 6305 of 1./Kampfgeschwader 55 'Greif-Geschwader' was shot up by fighters at midday on 25 September 1940 when returning from a bombing raid on the Bristol Aero Works. It crash-landed at Westhill Farm, near Swanage in Dorset, as shown here. All five crew members were taken prisoner but one was badly wounded and died.

J. Falconer collection

Wallace Nesbit, the author's younger brother, made a contribution to the country's economy by growing this enormous pumpkin on top of the air raid shelter in the garden of the family home at Woodford Green in Essex. It was fed with glucose and reached the weight of 84lb. After being wounded by a shell splinter it was presented to a local hospital and photographed by the local Press. Note the worn-out sole of Wallace's shoe. There were no repair facilities for civilians in the locality and it was not until Wallace joined the Auxiliary Fire Service that he became decently shod once more.

Wallace Nesbit collection

London was bombed again at night but with very few civilian casualties. Nine aircraft of the Luftflotten were lost and nine more damaged. Fighter Command lost seven aircraft (including a Hurricane which became lost and force-landed in Eire) with four more damaged but repairable.

The last day of September dawned bright but cloudy. Luftflotte 2 sent over two formations in the early morning but both were attacked with such ferocity that neither reached London. Luftflotte 3 tried to approach the south coast in mid-morning with a formation of bomb-carrying Bf110s escorted by Bf109 fighters, but received similar treatment. Another formation from Luftflotte 2 at midday was attacked over Kent, but some bombers got through to London. Luftflotte 3 tried once more, when a large formation of bombers and fighters approached the Westland factory at Yeovil but was thwarted by cloud and determined resistance from No. 10 Group. London was again attacked at night while other cities received nuisance attacks. Civilian casualties in all areas amounted to over 60 killed and 400 injured.

This was another dismal day for the Luftflotten, which lost forty-seven aircraft plus thirteen damaged. Fighter Command lost twenty-one aircraft in combat or accidents, plus twenty-three damaged but repairable. The German High Commanders, even including the self-opinionated and obtuse Goering, began at last to understand that daylight attacks over Britain were unprofitable. Fighter Command must have seemed like the mythical Hydra, which grew two heads for every one that was cut off.

This Junkers Ju88A, unit code 4D+AD of Gruppenstabstaffel, III./Kampfgeschwader 30 'Adler Geschwader', was flown by the Gruppenkommandeur, Major Hackbarth, during an attack on London Docks in the late afternoon of 9 September 1940. It was shot down by RAF fighters and crashed in the sea near Pagham in Sussex. The pilot and one other crew member were killed and the other two captured. The machine was a total loss.

Author's collection

The squadron badge of 303 (Polish) Squadron, which was formed with Hurricane Is at Northolt in Middlesex on 22 July 1940, from pilots and personnel of 1 (Warsaw) Squadron who had fought in Poland and France. The squadron became operational during the next month and by the time this photograph was taken had claimed 126 enemy aircraft shot down.

J. Falconer collection

The Messerschmitt Bf109E-4 of Oberleutnant Franz von Werra, the Gruppenadjutant of Stab II./Jagdgeschwader 3. It was damaged and then force-landed at Love's Farm, Marden in Kent, during a fighter sweep on 5 September 1940. Von Werra achieved fame by escaping from a train taking a group of Luftwaffe airmen to a PoW camp in Canada and then reaching the USA before that country entered the war. He managed to return to Germany but failed to return from a patrol over the North Sea.

Bruce Robertson collection

'ACHTUNG, SPITFEUER!'
by Charles J. Thompson
A Spitfire breaking away from attacking a Heinkel He111 over Essex in the Battle of Britain, viewed through the glazed and curved nose of another Heinkel He111. The seat in the 'glasshouse' nose was an exposed position for the German gunner/navigator, and there were serious problems with reflection when the sun was behind the bomber.

The headquarters of London's Anti-Aircraft
Barrage, deep underground. The Army officers
watched the counters showing enemy aircraft
formations plotted by girls of the Auxiliary
Territorial Service (ATS) and issued instructions
to their units, giving heights of fire and the type
of shells to be used. All Britain's anti-aircraft
defences, including the Observer Corps and
Balloon Command, worked in close and
instantaneous collaboration with the
headquarters of Fighter Command.

Author's collection

Gunners of Anti-Aircraft Command with a gun predictor in 1940.

Bruce Robertson collection

scheme will be settled shortly, when Parliament has passed the War Damage Bill.

(3) If bombing has left you without any *ready cash*, because you have lost your job or cannot get to work to be paid or because you have been hurt, you can apply to the Assistance Board.

COMPENSATION FOR DAMAGE TO HOUSES

IF YOU *own your house* or hold it on a long lease and it is damaged or destroyed, whatever your income, you should, as soon as possible, make a claim on Form V.O.W.1.* The amount of your compensation and the time of paying it will depend on the passing of the War Damage Bill now before Parliament.

REPAIRS

IF YOUR HOUSE can be made fit to live in with a few simple repairs the local authority (apply to the Borough or Council Engineer) will put it right if the landlord is not able to do it. But how quickly the local authority can do this depends on local conditions.

FOOD

IF YOU should find it more convenient not to do your own cooking or you are unable to get gas, water or electricity, then in a rapidly increasing number of places you will find both before and after the raid community kitchens. Here you can get well cooked, hot meals at low prices in cheerful surroundings. If you prefer to do so you can buy the food ready cooked and take it home.

* You can get this form at your Town Hall or the offices of your Council.

4

You can find out if there are community kitchens in your town and where they are from any policeman, from the Town Hall or Council offices or the Citizens' Advice Bureaux.

THE INJURED

IF YOU are injured, treatment will be given at First Aid Posts and Hospitals, and :—

(a) If your doctor says you are unable to work as a result of a "war injury," you will be eligible to receive an *injury allowance*. Application should be made immediately to the local office of the Assistance Board and you should take with you, or send, a medical certificate from a doctor or a hospital.

(b) If you are afterwards found to be suffering from a serious and prolonged disablement, your case will be considered for a disability pension.

(c) Widows of workers and Civil Defence Volunteers killed on duty will receive £2 10s. 0d. a week for ten weeks, after which a widow's pension will become payable. Pensions for orphans and dependent parents are also provided.

Ask at the Post Office for the address of the local branch of the Ministry of Pensions if you want to apply for a pension.

KEEP THIS AND DO WHAT IT TELLS YOU. HELP IS WAITING FOR YOU. THE GOVERNMENT, YOUR FELLOW CITIZENS AND YOUR NEIGHBOURS WILL SEE THAT "FRONT LINE" FIGHTERS ARE LOOKED AFTER !

Issued by the Ministry of Home Security in co-operation with the following Departments: The Treasury, the Ministry of Health, the Ministry of Pensions, the Ministry of Food and the Assistance Board.

5/-8415 (3) N. & Co.   5

AFTER THE RAID

ISSUED BY THE MINISTRY OF HOME SECURITY
PROVINCIAL EDITION   DECEMBER, 1940

AFTER THE RAID

WHEN YOU HAVE been in the front line and taken it extra hard the country wants to look after you. For you have suffered in the national interest as well as in your own in the fight against Hitler. If your home is damaged there is a great deal of help ready for you.

You will want to know where this help can be found and whom to ask about it. Here are some hints about how you stand. Remember, in reading them, that conditions are different in different areas and the services may not always be quite the same.

HAVE YOUR PLANS READY

YOU SHOULD TRY to make plans *now* to go and stay with friends or relations living near, but not too near, *in case your house is destroyed*. They should also arrange *now* to come to you if their house is knocked out.

If you have to go and stay with them until you can make more permanent arrangements the Government will pay them a lodging allowance of 5s. per week for each adult and 3s. for each child. Your host should enquire at the Town Hall or Council offices about this.

Find out now, in case of emergency, from the police or wardens where the offices are at which the local authority and the Assistance Board are, doing their work for people who have been bombed.

1

FOOD AND SHELTER

IF YOU HAVE NOT been able to make arrangements with friends or relatives and have *nowhere to sleep and eat* after your house has been destroyed, the best thing to do is to go to an emergency *Rest Centre*. The wardens and policemen will tell you where this is. You will get food and shelter there until you can go home or make other arrangements. You will also find at the Rest Centre an officer whose job it is to help you with your problems. He will tell you how to get *clothes* if you've lost your own, *money* —if you are in need—a new ration book, a new identity card, a new gas mask, etc.

NEW HOMES FOR THE HOMELESS

A HOME WILL BE FOUND for you, if you cannot make your own arrangements. If you are still earning your normal wages you may have to pay rent.

If you can make arrangements to go and stay with friends or relatives, you will be given a free travel voucher if you cannot get to them without help. Enquire about this at the Rest Centre.

TRACING FRIENDS AND RELATIVES

TO KEEP IN TOUCH with your friends and relatives you should, if you find your own accommodation, send your new address to the Secretary, London Council of Social Service, 7, Bayley Street, Bedford Square, London, W.C.1. Of course, also tell your friends and relatives where you are.

2

Anyone who is homeless and has been provided with accommodation can be found through the Town Halls, the Council offices and the Citizens' Advice Bureaux, since records are kept.

If you have got sons or daughters in the Army, Navy, R.A.F., or the Auxiliary Services, they can find you, too, through their Commanding Officer, wherever you may be, whether you have gone to the country, are in hospital or are with friends.

FURNITURE AND OTHER BELONGINGS

(1) If your income is below a certain amount you can apply to the Assistance Board for :—

(a) a grant to replace *essential* furniture* and *essential* household articles ;

(b) a grant to replace your clothes† or those of your family ;

(c) a grant to replace *tools*† essential to your work.

You also have a claim for your other belongings, but these do not come under the Assistance Board's scheme, and you should make your claim on Form V.O.W.1.‡

(2) If your income is above certain limits you do not come under the Assistance Board's scheme and should make out a claim for all your belongings on Form V.O.W 1.‡

The time at which payment can be made for belongings not covered by the Assistance Board's

* The household income must normally £400 a year or less (i.e., nearly £8 0s. 0d. per week or less).
† Your income in this case must be normally £250 a year or less (i.e., nearly £5 0s. 0d. per week or less) or £400 a year or less if you have dependants.
‡ You can get this form at your Town Hall or the offices of your Council.

3

The area around St Paul's in the City of London during the Blitz which began on 7/8 September 1940 and continued until 10/11 May 1941. Sappers were carrying out blasting operations, blowing down the walls of burnt-out buildings which had been rendered unsafe.

Author's collection

Bomb damage in New Road, Littlehampton, Sussex.

Bruce Robertson collection

One of the Czechoslovak pilots of 312 Squadron, a talented violinist, entertains fellow pilots in the squadron crew room at RAF Speke in Lancashire. Some of the men are kitted ready for flying, evidently on standby duties.

Author's collection

Some Czechoslovak pilots who flew with the French Air Force escaped to Britain where they formed 312 Squadron on 29 August 1940. Equipped with Hurricane Is, this squadron was sent on 26 September 1940 from Duxford in Cambridgeshire to Speke in Lancashire, where this photograph was taken. The main duties were to defend Merseyside against enemy air attack.

Author's collection

An armoured car silhouetted against the sky while patrolling the south-east coast of England during the Battle of Britain, ready to fire at low-flying German aircraft.

Author's collection

Oberleutnant Karl Fisher of 7./Jagdgeschwader 27 force-landed his damaged Messerschmitt Bf109E-1, White 9, near Queen Anne's Gate in Windsor Great Park on 30 September 1940, after combat with RAF fighters when escorting a bomber formation. His machine overturned but was righted by the RAF and put on display in the local high street. Fisher was uninjured and taken prisoner.

Author's collection

The German groundcrew has worked at night to prepare this Heinkel He111H-1 for another sortie. The aircraft, camouflaged black, is now fully bombed up and refuelled, and the crew members are putting on their flying gear. The pilot is being helped into his lightweight suit while another crew member ties up his kapok-filled lifejacket.

Jean-Louis Roba collection

The memorial stone near Church Farm, Woolverton in Somerset, to Sergeant Kenneth C.H. Ripley, a pilot of 152 Squadron based at Warmwell in Dorset, who was shot down in Spitfire I serial N3173 on 25 September 1940 during a combat with Heinkel He111s attacking the Bristol Aero Works.

J. Falconer collection

Firemen dousing buildings on 28 September 1940, after a night in which several large fires were started in London and there were heavy casualties in the St Pancras district.

Bruce Robertson collection

Air Raid Wardens were issued with hand-operated stirrup pumps intended mainly to deal with minor fires caused by incendiary bombs. The base of the cylinder was placed in a bucket of water. One warden pumped while another directed a spray of water at the fire and a third replenished the bucket.

Bruce Robertson collection

Pilot and gunner climbing into their Blenheim IF of 29 Squadron during the Luftwaffe's night attacks. This mark of Blenheim was fitted with a gun-pack containing four .303in Brownings as extra forward-firing armament. This squadron pioneered the first airborne interception radar used for night-fighting, although it was in Beaufighters that the major successes were scored, from 19 November 1940.

J. Falconer collection

A Gefreiter (Leading Aircraftman) after capture. His boots and socks have been taken off by his captors, to prevent any attempt to escape. They are on top of his parachute, which is partly open, possibly having been picked up in error by the D-ring.

Author's collection

Junkers Ju88A-1 coded 3Z+DK of 2./Kampfgeschwader 77 was damaged by anti-aircraft fire and fighter attack in the afternoon of 30 September 1940, during a bombing sortie against London. It force-landed at Gatwick racecourse in Surrey, with one crew member dead and three wounded. The wreckage was taken to the Royal Aircraft Establishment for examination and later exhibited to the public at Primrose Hill in London.

Philip Jarrett collection

CHAPTER EIGHT

THE END OF
THE BATTLE

'Victory has many fathers. Defeat is an orphan.'

Attr. John F. Kennedy

Bomber Command continued its operations at night after the attack on Berlin of 23/24 September, the main targets being ports harbouring invasion barges. These attacks were carried out on an almost nightly basis until 13 October, when it became apparent that an invasion would not be mounted until the following spring, if at all. The ports were far easier targets than those inland. The distances were shorter and it was easy to pick out the docks from the air on fairly clear nights. Crews in the Operational Training Units were sometimes added to the bomber streams on these tasks, and losses were usually quite low. For instance, there were no losses at all on 12/13 October when ninety-three bombers were despatched to targets on the Channel coast and in Germany. No attempts were made in this period to resume the costly practice of daylight attacks.

The heavy losses of the Luftflotten in the three months up to the end of September also resulted in a change of policy. Daylight attacks continued on a lesser scale and most of these were carried out at higher altitudes, where the escorting Messerschmitt Bf109s enjoyed a better performance than either Spitfires or Hurricanes. Moreover at 20,000ft or more the enemy formations were difficult to track by either the RDF stations or the Observer Corps. At night these bombers usually flew above the level where the searchlights and anti-aircraft batteries were at their most effective, although their bombing was often inaccurate as a result.

By early October Fighter Command had rebuilt some of it strength and was reaching full establishment, but its night-fighter squadrons were still woefully equipped. Two Defiant squadrons, one in Lancashire and the other in Scotland, had some success. After being vectored on to an intruder, the tactic involved flying below and looking up into the night sky where there was a better chance of spotting it. The four guns in the turret could then blast the belly of an enemy. Hurricanes were sometimes employed at night, but without the assistance of an air observer or any special equipment the pilot had his hands full merely trying to fly the fighter, let alone hunt for the enemy. The airborne interception equipment in the six Blenheim squadrons was inadequate. However, a more advanced device, the A.I. Mark VI, was being produced and would be fitted in the new Bristol Beaufighter. This was a much faster and more powerful machine, with the benefit of four 20mm cannons in the nose and six .303in machine-guns in the wings. But the first victory scored by this new night-fighter did not come until 19 November, when a Junkers Ju88 was shot down by an aircraft of 604 Squadron. Meanwhile the casualty rate of the German night bomber force over Britain ran at less than 1 per cent, an average at which the campaign could be sustained indefinitely.

The morning of 1 October was fine, with some clouds. In mid-morning a force of about a hundred aircraft from Luftflotte 3 approached Southampton and Portsmouth. They were mostly Bf110s carrying bombs, escorted by Bf109s, flying at high level in accordance with the change in tactics. Some of the single-engined Bf109s had been converted to carry a small bomb-load, although accuracy from such altitudes was non-existent. Spitfires and Hurricanes climbed up to meet them. Luftflotte 2 also sent formations over south-east England from the early afternoon, with bombs dropping on London. The capital was also raided at night, while smaller formations headed for Liverpool, Manchester and Glasgow. Civilian casualties during the day in all areas were reported as 67 killed and over 300 injured. The Luftflotten lost twelve aircraft in operations or accidents, plus two damaged, while Fighter Command lost six plus two damaged but repairable.

There was similar weather on the next day, when several formations from Luftflotte 2 operated over Biggin Hill and London during the morning, fiercely opposed by Fighter Command. The night raiders made their usual attacks on London and other cities. In all, 24 civilians were reported killed, plus 170 injured. German losses amounted to eighteen aircraft written off and three damaged, while Fighter Command lost only two aircraft, with one pilot injured, plus three damaged but repairable. Rain and low clouds restricted operations on 3 October but some bombers reached London and other cities during the night. Some 70 civilians were reported killed and almost 240 injured. The Germans lost nine aircraft, with four more damaged, while Fighter Command lost one Spitfire plus four aircraft damaged but repairable.

Rain and mist persisted on 4 October but there were two attacks on convoys and a steady stream of small formations headed for London, which was also the target for most of the night attacks. In all, 69 civilians were killed, mostly in London, and 286 injured. Fifteen German aircraft were lost during the day, with seven damaged, while Fighter Command lost only one, with four damaged but repairable. Park issued instructions to counter daylight attacks at high level by requiring Group controllers, if time permitted, to get the Spitfires in readiness at 25,000ft and the Hurricanes at 20,000ft before vectoring them on to the enemy, either in pairs or in wings.

There was mixed weather on 5 October but attacks by fairly small formations came over from the two Luftflotten and were intercepted. Detling, Folkestone, London and Southampton were all attacked. Docks in London and the East End were set alight by bombs and incendiaries during the night. A total of 66 civilians were killed in all areas throughout the day and night, with over 300 injured. Fourteen German aircraft were destroyed and eleven damaged, while Fighter Command lost seven plus eleven damaged but repairable. There was rainy weather on 6 October, but Biggin Hill and Middle Wallop were attacked during the day. In all, 23 civilians were killed during daylight hours, plus almost 100 injured, but rain and low cloud restricted the attacks at night and there were no

casualties. The Luftflotten lost nine aircraft and four damaged, while Fighter Command lost two plus three damaged but repairable.

The weather was somewhat better on 7 October and the Luftflotten sent over a series of small formations during the day, the main targets being Biggin Hill and the Westland aircraft factory at Yeovil in Somerset. There were numerous raids at night, mostly against London and Merseyside, but bombs were also dropped on various airfields. The day resulted in 31 civilian deaths plus about 170 injured. The Luftflotten lost nineteen aircraft, with eight damaged. Fighter Command had a bad day with seventeen aircraft lost and eight damaged but repairable. On this day Goering announced a plan in which he proposed the obliteration of London and the demoralisation of its civilians, coupled with the paralysing of Britain's commercial and industrial life. This was more 'wishful thinking' on the part of the Luftwaffe's leader. His plan might have been more appropriate as a forecast of Germany's future.

The weather was cloudy but fair on 8 October. Formations came over in the early morning and succeeded in dropping bombs on the centre of London and the City, causing considerable damage and casualties. A steady stream of bombers arrived at night, London being the main target once again. Civilian casualties were heavy, with 225 killed and over 450 injured. The Luftflotten did not fare too well, losing sixteen aircraft plus fifteen damaged, while Fighter Command wrote off eight aircraft with four more damaged but repairable. London was a target once more during the next day, while some airfields received accurate

Unteroffizier H. Bley being brought ashore by the Dungeness lifeboat on 7 October 1940 after his Messerschmitt Bf109E-4 of 4./Jagdgeschwader 2 had been brought down in the sea about 2 miles off Greatstone-on-Sea in Kent during a combat with RAF fighters. Bley's head is bandaged from a wound sustained in the crash.

Bruce Robertson collection

(Overleaf) 'ATTACK ON WESTLANDS' by Mark Postlethwaite
On 7 October 1940 a force of Junkers Ju88s, escorted by Messerschmitt Bf109s and Bf110s, made an attack on the Westland aircraft factory at Yeovil in Somerset. This Junkers Ju88A-1 was on the strength of Kampfgeschwader 51 (Edelweiss-Geschwader).

bombing. There was a heavy raid on the capital during the night. During both day and night raids, civilian casualties amounted to 100 dead and over 400 injured. German losses amounted to ten aircraft, with thirteen more damaged, while Fighter Command lost three, with two more damaged but repairable.

On 10 October small formations in steady streams penetrated the British defences and bombed various targets, including London. The capital was attacked once more at night, as were Liverpool, Manchester and some airfields. The Home Office did not report civilian casualties for this day. The Luftflotten lost twelve aircraft plus eleven damaged, while Fighter Command lost eight, with two damaged but repairable. The next day saw much the same pattern of attacks, with ten German aircraft lost and seven damaged, while Fighter Command losses were eight aircraft written off plus eight damaged but repairable. Civilian casualties were over 50 killed and 250 injured.

St Paul's Cathedral during the Blitz on London.
Bruce Robertson collection

Attacks continued on 12 October, mainly against the capital at night but with smaller raids on Birmingham and Coventry. Almost 100 civilians were killed and over 400 injured. The day cost the Luftflotten thirteen aircraft, with another damaged, while Fighter Command lost eleven in operations or accidents, plus five more damaged but repairable. These harassing attacks continued on 13 October, with the centre of London bombed in the afternoon and at night. Liverpool, Birkenhead, Birmingham and Bristol were also raided. Civilian deaths were reported as 233 killed and almost 200 injured, but in addition about 200 people were buried in a basement when a block of flats in London collapsed on them. Six German aircraft were lost, plus six damaged, while Fighter Command lost four with four more damaged but repairable.

Meanwhile Hitler had issued no further orders about a date for the invasion. He had decided that the best way to eliminate Britain was by a combination of night bombing and U-boat operations, with the purpose of starving the country into submission. His thoughts were now concentrated on an invasion of Russia, although it was not until 18 December 1940 that he issued his first directive for Operation Barbarossa.

There was a continuation of widespread but small attacks during daylight on 14 October. The East End of London was bombed once again, and the West End also received some damage during the night attacks. About 200 people were reported killed and over 800 injured. Only four German aircraft were lost while six were damaged. Fighter Command lost one aircraft plus four damaged but repairable. The next day brought attacks on the centre of London and the City, and these were followed by an extremely heavy raid in the full moon period at night. Almost 300 people were killed and nearly 1,300 injured during the day, mostly in London. The Luftflotten lost sixteen aircraft during the day plus eleven damaged. It was not a good day for Fighter Command, which wrote off fifteen aircraft, including one destroyed on the ground, plus seventeen damaged but repairable.

Fog kept most German aircraft grounded during daylight on 16 October, but there were attacks on London at night. Civilian casualties amounted to over 70 killed and almost 300 injured, mostly during the night bombing of London. The Luftflotten lost fifteen aircraft while seven more were damaged, mostly in accidents during bad weather. Fighter Command lost three aircraft, of which two were in accidents, plus four damaged but repairable. Visibility improved enough during the next day for a combination of Bf110s and Bf109s to raid Margate and Broadstairs, followed by more attacks in central London. London, Liverpool and Birmingham were the main targets at night. Civilian casualties reported during the day and night were over 130 killed and 525 injured, with London the worst affected. Sixteen German aircraft were written off and eight damaged, whereas Fighter Command wrote off three plus two damaged but repairable.

Fog also reduced activity on 18 October during both day and night. There were only scattered raids by intruders, but 58 civilians were killed and over 200 injured. The Luftflotten wrote off fourteen aircraft, mainly from accidents in bad weather, with ten more damaged. Fighter Command lost six in accidents, with six more damaged but repairable. There was some improvement in weather conditions during the next day, resulting in fighter-bomber attacks on London, followed by some night raids on the capital, Liverpool, Bristol and the Midlands. Reported casualties were nearly 200 killed and 625 injured, mostly in the capital. The Luftflotten lost six aircraft, with three more damaged, while Fighter Command wrote off two aircraft in accidents, with three more damaged but repairable. The failure of night-fighters to score victories was causing concern. Although the Beaufighter I had begun to enter service in replacement for the Blenheim IF, there were delays in converting on to the machine, the crews needed more practice with the new RDF equipment on board and ground control was not yet adequate.

On 20 October raiders penetrated inland at high level during the day but the worst attacks were at night when London was hit badly and the Midlands received scattered raids. Nearly 150 civilian deaths were reported, with about 550 injured. Eleven German aircraft were lost, with the same number damaged, while Fighter Command wrote off four, with four more damaged but repairable. In cloudy weather during the next day small formations penetrated inland to London and Liverpool, followed by widespread raids at night on London, Liverpool and cities in the Midlands. The trickle of losses continued with seven German aircraft written off and seven more damaged, while Fighter Command lost only two, with one more damaged but repairable. The grim total of civilian casualties continued, with about 75 killed and 740 injured. There was much the same pattern on 22 October, with a fairly quiet morning followed by the arrival of enemy formations in the afternoon, and then small raids on London, Liverpool and Coventry at night. The civilian death toll was lighter at 35, with about 150 injured. The Luftflotten lost twelve aircraft, with seven more damaged, while Fighter Command's losses amounted to six aircaft written off and two damaged but repairable.

There was a very quiet day on 23 October, with low clouds and rain, but London and Glasgow received some bombs at night. The Luftflotten lost only four aircraft, with three more damaged, while a Blenheim of Fighter Command crashed accidentally and a Spitfire was damaged but repairable. Civilian casualties were 24 killed and about 50 injured. Another quiet day followed, with nuisance raids in daylight followed by attacks on London and Birmingham at night. Only 2 people were reported killed, plus 60 injured. German losses were

A heavy anti-aircraft battery, based in London's
Hyde Park, in action at night in 1940.

Author's collection

twelve aircraft, with four more damaged, while Fighter Command lost four aircraft in accidents and three more damaged but repairable.

The pace hotted up on 25 October with fighter-bomber attacks in daylight, but the night was notable for the first raids made by units of the Regia Aeronautica which had moved to Belgium. This raid was Mussolini's response to the RAF's bombing of Italy, but it achieved little at the cost of three machines which failed to return. London, Liverpool and Birmingham were attacked once more by the Luftflotten at night, and civilian casualties amounted to over 200 killed and 550 injured. German losses were heavier than usual, with twenty-four aircraft written off and fourteen damaged. Fighter Command lost fourteen aircraft, with eight more damaged but repairable. The pressure continued during the next day, with the usual fighter-bomber attacks during the shortening daylight hours followed by a heavy raid on London and others on Liverpool, Manchester and various cities in the Midlands. Civilian casualties were about 165 killed and 475 injured. The day cost the Luftflotten ten aircraft lost and fourteen damaged, while Fighter Command lost eight plus four damaged but repairable.

The morning of 27 October was cloudy but both Luftflotten made an early raid on London and the docks in the East End. More raids followed in the afternoon and the capital received its usual quota at night. Liverpool and Bristol were also bombed. Reported civilian deaths were about 60 killed and 150 injured. Sixteen German aircraft were lost, while fourteen more were damaged; Fighter Command had a relatively bad day with fourteen aircraft written off and three damaged but repairable. Fog reduced activities during the following morning but air battles took place in the afternoon and there were widespread night raids. The day resulted in about 70 civilian deaths, plus about 350 injured. The balance of losses swung back against the Luftflotten, with fourteen aircraft destroyed and six damaged, whereas Fighter Command had only two aircraft damaged but repairable.

With the days getting steadily shorter, the Luftflotten made a determined effort on 29 October. Fighters and bombers from Luftflotte 2 poured over during the morning and there were fierce air battles with Spitfires and Hurricanes. Luftflotte 3 attacked Portsmouth in the afternoon while aircraft of the Regia Aeronautica raided Ramsgate. London received its usual nightly visits and there were other raids over the Midlands. Reported civilian casualties were about 40 killed and over 150 injured. But it was a costly day for the attackers, with twenty-eight aircraft lost and four damaged, while Fighter Command lost eight plus eleven damaged but repairable. The next day brought reduced activity, partly because the weather began closing in, but both Luftflotten sent over smaller formations during the day. Civilian deaths were fewer than usual at 15, but about 220 people were injured. Eight German aircraft were lost and ten damaged. Fighter Command lost nine aircraft, mainly in accidents, with seven others damaged but repairable. The final day of the month brought some fighter and fighter-bomber sweeps in rainy weather, but almost no night raids. Only 21 civilian deaths were reported, with about 125 injured. Aircraft losses were light, with only three German aircraft destroyed and three damaged, while two aircraft of Fighter Command were slightly damaged in accidents.

Young women of the Auxiliary Territorial Service (ATS) working at night on an identification telescope, giving the bearing and elevation of an aircraft.

Author's collection

The end of October 1940 is when Dowding and British air historians consider the Battle of Britain came to an end. German air historians take a different view. They believe it is more accurate to date the end to the middle of May 1941, when the first Blitz against Britain petered out. From this date most of the units of the Luftwaffe were withdrawn to the Eastern Front in preparation for Operation Barbarossa, the invasion of Russia. (In fact German air historians seldom use the term 'Battle of Britain' but instead prefer a title such as 'The Intensification of the Air War against Britain'.)

On 7 June 1945 the Senior Narrator of the RAF's Air Historical Branch addressed a lengthy questionnaire on the subject of the Battle of Britain to two senior German officers who had survived the war, Generalfeldmarschall Milch and Generalleutnant Galland. Both were completely frank and forthcoming in their answers. Galland also amplified his remarks in his autobiography *The First and the Last*, published in Germany in 1953.

Milch believed that the main reason for the deferment of the beginning of the air assault against Britain was Hitler's offer of peace on 19 July 1940, which he expected would be accepted. After its contemptuous rejection, the two officers believed that the plan for invasion under Operation Sealion would have been carried out, provided air superiority over the Channel could have been obtained. The targets attacked by the bombers were of secondary importance to bringing Fighter Command to battle and eliminating it as an effective force. Some of the targets such as the airfields were well chosen, but attacks on London itself were made primarily as a further means of achieving combat with RAF fighters. Neither commander appeared to appreciate how crucial the RDF stations were to the defence of Britain, but they considered these were difficult targets to attack.

Both commanders commented on the failure of the Junkers Ju87 and stated that it could not be used where it met fighter opposition; it had to be withdrawn in August and thereafter played no part. Both agreed that the root fault of the Luftwaffe was the short range of the Messerschmitt Bf109. The twin-engined Bf110 was a disappointing aircraft and no substitute for it. The Bf109s had to link up quickly with the bomber component if they were to have enough fuel to accompany them and then fight inland. The chances of doing so were poor in cloudy weather because the bomber crews had no suitable R/T equipment for communicating with their fighter escorts.

Although not discussed in this interrogation, it may be worth commenting on the failure of the Luftwaffe to provide drop-tanks for the Bf109. Certainly the Germans were experienced in the use of such auxiliary tanks. For example, the Heinkel He51B-1 biplane was fitted with a 170-litre drop-tank beneath the fuselage when employed in the Spanish Civil War. German drop-tanks were found in various parts of Britain during the Battle. A document in the Public Record Office contains a report on one from the police in Nottingham, dated 29 August 1940; it is described as a 'wooden shaped bomb' built of plywood glued together and containing traces of petrol. Others were reported at different times in Cambridge, Norfolk, Edinburgh and the Isle of Wight. But none of these was carried by the Bf109E, the principal variant employed in the Battle of Britain, even though many of these machines were converted to the fighter-bomber role and carried a 250kg bomb.

The Bf109E was fitted with a 400-litre fuel tank behind the pilot's seat. Making an allowance for start-up and take-off, this gave a theoretical range of 286 miles, or 55 minutes, at maximum continuous rpm and at an altitude of 16,000ft. Alternatively, the most economical cruise setting at the same altitude gave a range of 413 miles, or an endurance of 1 hour 50 minutes. But these figures bore no relation to operational conditions in the Battle of Britain. Assembling over a rendezvous point usually took about 30 minutes. When the fighters escorted the slower Heinkel He111s they had to weave behind them, using up so much fuel that they had to turn back after reaching the outskirts of south London. In his book Galland mentions that the Bf109s usually had only about twelve minutes of time available for combat over England.

The problem of converting the machines was technically very difficult. The Bf109s had no shackles or fuel leads which would allow the carrying of a 300-litre drop-tank, known as a Junkers/NKF. Although the bomb racks on the E-1/B and E/4B fighter-bomber variants could have been converted, the intricate installation of internal fuel and air pressure lines, with pumps and valves, was far too complicated. The Bf109E-7 long-range fighter-bomber, carrying a drop-tank, was developed in late August 1940, but its production in large numbers was too late for the Battle of Britain. Had it been available, the situation over Britain could have been transformed.

The two commanders were unanimous in stating that the Luftwaffe threw all it could into this battle. Every available fighter was employed, but these could escort only a limited number of bombers. British fighter opposition proved far stronger than anticipated. Galland had been assured by German Intelligence that Fighter Command was so badly weakened that only about a hundred aircraft were left, yet they still came up in undiminished strength. The switch to night bombing was the result of heavy German losses in daylight, although neither commander could remember the exact casualty figures.

Air historians differ about German casualty figures, perhaps because those killed in accidents are sometimes not included. Men who were wounded but got back in damaged machines may have died later, and some of those who came down in Britain may also have died of their wounds. German records are incomplete. Perhaps the most authoritative book on this subject is the monumental work *The Battle of Britain Then and Now*, published by After the Battle in 1980. The researchers who compiled this admirable study give the total number of Luftwaffe airmen killed as 2,662, compared with the well-known figure of 537 RAF airmen killed.

Those who flew in the Battle of Britain and have survived to this day are now old men, but they still have vivid memories. Although the period from 10 July to 31 October was not long for a single operational tour in the wartime RAF, some of the men had been in action without a break since the German assault on the west. Moreover, the intensity of flying, physical tiredness and high level of casualties must have imposed a great strain on those who flew in this period. Yet by all accounts there was never any loss of morale. In spite of casualties, RAF messes were not gloomy places. The men were full of life, fun-loving, perhaps boisterous at times, mostly keen on sport and proud to be in the forefront of the best technology of the age. They were young and physically fit, of a high standard of education, and all were volunteers for flying duties. Their motives were certainly not related to financial rewards. The pay of a sergeant in the General Duties (i.e. Flying) Branch of the RAF was 12*s* 6*d* a day in 1940. A pilot officer received 14*s* 6*d* a day, out of which he had to pay his mess bills. Such sums seem derisory today but they were adequate at the time, although less than the pay of a skilled factory worker. Of course the men were buoyed up by public approbation as well as the knowledge that they were winning the battle and that the survival of the country and perhaps the whole of the free world depended upon them.

While these Battle of Britain heroes received the acclamation of the country for their victory, their leader was given short shrift. On 25 October 1940 Air Chief Marshal Sir Charles Portal had been appointed as Chief of the Air Staff, in replacement for Sir Cyril Newall, who retired as a Marshal of the Royal Air Force. One of Portal's decisions was to remove Air Chief Marshal Sir Hugh Dowding from his position as Air Officer Commanding-in-Chief of Fighter Command. This post was taken over on 25 November 1940 by Air Marshal Sir W. Sholto Douglas, transferred from his position as Deputy Chief of Air Staff. In turn Douglas decided that Air Vice-Marshal Keith Park should be 'rested' and removed from his position as commander of No. 11 Group. On 18 December 1940 Park was sent to command

Hitler visiting the Messerschmitt Works in late 1940. Left to right: Brigade Leader Theo Croneiss; the engineer Fritz Hentzen; Hitler; Generaloberst Ernst Udet; Willy Messerschmitt; Rakan Kokothaki. Udet was one of the most famous and experienced German pilots. He was a hero in the First World War, with sixty-two kills to his credit, and a stunt pilot afterwards. In June 1935 he joined the Luftwaffe with the rank of Oberst. On 1 February 1939 he was made Generalluftzeugmeister (Master-General of Air Material) in control of the Technical Department, which consisted of twenty-five sections, but he proved unequal to the task. He was responsible for the Luftwaffe's acceptance of the Messerschmitt Bf109 as its standard single-engined fighter. After the Luftwaffe's failure in the Battle of Britain, much of the blame was laid at his door. He became seriously depressed, both mentally and physically ill, and shot himself on 17 November 1941, at the age of 45. Hitler represented his death as 'an accident while testing a new weapon' and ordered a state funeral.

Bruce Robertson collection

Patients being evacuated from a hospital in the London area after it was hit for the third time by night raiders. There is a gaping hole in the background, where one wing has been completely demolished.

Author's collection

No. 23 Flying Training Group at South Cerney in Gloucestershire. He was replaced by his main critic, Air Vice-Marshal Trafford Leigh-Mallory.

It has been asserted that these changes in command stemmed from a meeting at the Air Ministry on 17 October 1940, convened by Sholto Douglas and attended by senior officers who included Dowding, Park and Leigh-Mallory. Also present was the commanding officer of 242 Squadron, Squadron Leader Douglas Bader. During this meeting the controversy over the 'Big Wing' issue came to a head. It was perhaps surprising that Bader, a relatively junior officer among a gathering of officers of air rank, was allowed to advocate the employment of Big Wings so forcefully.

Arguments over the merits of the Big Wings in the Battle of Britain have raged since this meeting and still occur today. It is obvious to any airman with experience of operational flying that a wing of five squadrons, each consisting of twelve fighters, is capable of shooting down more enemy aircraft than two squadrons. However, it is also evident that such a wing could miss much of the enemy force if the latter split into several formations and made for different targets. It is also clear that if the wing took longer to assemble, as it usually did, it might miss the enemy altogether, at least on its initial bombing run. Another obvious factor is that No. 11 Group usually had less time to assemble a wing than No. 12 Group, simply because it was nearer the approaching enemy.

According to one of the controllers of No. 11 Group this matter was put to the test in early 1941 when Leigh-Mallory decided to recreate the circumstances of one of the actual attacks in the Battle of Britain, and respond by assembling two Big Wings, in a mock battle. One squadron at each station was put at immediate readiness, another at fifteen minutes' availability and a third at thirty minutes. The decision of the umpires was that the enemy formations had bombed Biggin Hill and Kenley and were on their way back home before the Wings could intercept them.

However, the decision to replace Dowding and Park was unlikely to have been influenced unduly by the Big Wing controversy. There can be little doubt that Dowding and Park needed a rest after the tremendous strain of command in this period. More importantly, Dowding did not fit into the future conduct of the war as envisaged by the War Cabinet. Having won the Battle of Britain, the country must go over to the offensive, if only to demonstrate to the USA that it was capable of doing so. The army was not capable of mounting an attack on the European mainland, except with small Commando raids, but it could smash the Italians in East Africa and North Africa. The Royal Navy was at full stretch combating enemy U-boats and the threats from capital ships. But the RAF could be built up to deliver stupendous blows against the enemy. All three fighting commands must participate in this great endeavour. Bomber Commmand should wreck the German heartland with its new four-engined bombers while Coastal Command should form strike squadrons to sink coastal shipping and raid enemy ports. Fighter Command should also go over to the offensive, with improved variants of Spitfires escorting small formations of bombers in daylight and bringing enemy fighters to battle. Dowding, the great expert on the defensive role, was considered unsuitable for this task. Sholto Douglas and Leigh-Mallory were men who longed for the offensive, as did Portal.

Even though his removal may have hurt, Dowding accepted the decision with good grace. For him it was the winning of the Battle of Britain which mattered, not his own position. He was always fiercely protective and supportive of the men who served under him in the squadrons. When the king appointed him Knight Grand Commander of the Bath on 30 September 1940, he said that perhaps it should be split into a thousand parts and distributed among his

Pilots who flew in the Battle of Britain staging a scramble at RAF Biggin Hill on 14 September 1946, for a television programme. The Spitfire IXs were on the strength of 129 Squadron.

Aeroplane

'fighter boys'. Certainly he bore no resentment against Bader for his forthright comments on 17 October.

The question of what to do with the RAF's most senior Air Chief Marshal must have vexed the Air Ministry. At the suggestion of Lord Beaverbrook, he was sent across the North Atlantic, partly to persuade the Americans to manufacture the Napier Sabre engine and to visit aircraft factories. He spent time in both the USA and Canada, helping with arrangements to ferry the Consolidated B-24 Liberator to Britain. On arrival back home in one of these machines in the late spring of 1941, he was asked to write a despatch on the Battle of Britain and told that he would be retired in the following October, at the age of 59.

Soon after his retirement was gazetted, he was asked by Churchill to act as an efficiency expert and to suggest how RAF establishments could be reduced satisfactorily. He accepted this appointment reluctantly and put forward numerous ideas for economies, most of which were opposed by the Air Ministry. He asked to be placed on the retired list, and this was accepted.

Relieved at last of his responsibilities, Dowding relaxed and mellowed. He became 1st Baron Dowding in 1943. Fortunately his son Derek survived the war. Casting around for a pursuit to interest him, Dowding developed a huge interest in spiritualism, becoming an author on this subject and a popular speaker. One of those who sought his advice was Muriel Whiting, the widow of Pilot Officer Jack Maxwell Whiting, a flight engineer who was one of six crew members lost when a Lancaster I of 630 Squadron failed to return from a mine-laying sortie on the night of 21/22 May 1944. Hugh Dowding and Muriel Whiting were married on

Air Chief Marshal Sir Hugh Dowding, Air Officer Commanding-in-Chief of Fighter Command. Lord Dowding died on 15 February 1970.

Author's collection

25 September 1951. They had a happy life and Dowding lived to the age of almost 88, although he was confined to a wheelchair when he attended the opening of the film *Battle of Britain* in 1969.

Among his peers in his service life Dowding could be cantankerous, a bad mixer and single-minded in his demands, and he probably seemed somewhat eccentric at times. These were characteristics not unknown in other British military commanders throughout the centuries. Whatever his personal defects, he out-manoeuvred Goering and the other senior Luftwaffe commanders with his superior intellect and knowledge of war in the air. Moreover, he was a man of integrity who invariably put his country before his own interests. In the rather old-fashioned but best sense of the word, he was a patriot.

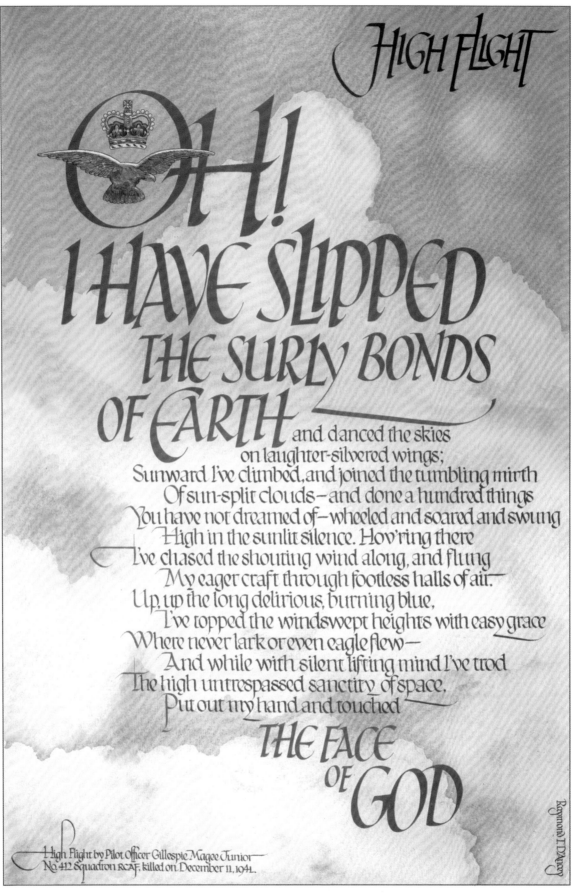

HIGH FLIGHT

OH! I HAVE SLIPPED THE SURLY BONDS OF EARTH and danced the skies
on laughter-silvered wings;
Sunward I've climbed, and joined the tumbling mirth
Of sun-split clouds—and done a hundred things
You have not dreamed of—wheeled and soared and swung
High in the sunlit silence. Hov'ring there
I've chased the shouting wind along, and flung
My eager craft through footless halls of air.
Up, up the long delirious, burning blue,
I've topped the windswept heights with easy grace
Where never lark or even eagle flew—
And while with silent lifting mind I've trod
The high untrespassed sanctity of space,
Put out my hand and touched THE FACE OF GOD

High Flight by Pilot Officer Gillespie Magee Junior
No. 412 Squadron RCAF, killed on December 11, 1941.

Raymond I D'Arcey

Pilot Officer Magee was an American who volunteered to serve in the Royal Canadian Air Force. He flew Spitfire VBs with 412 (RCAF) Squadron but was killed when the squadron was based at Wellingore in Lincolnshire. His Spitfire VB serial AD291 collided with an Airspeed Oxford from Cranwell during a cloud flying exercise. The poem was found in his effects.

Royal Air Force Museum L247/Calligraphy by Raymond D'Ancey

The young women of the ATS became adept at working with predictors and range-finders. They also drove and serviced the trucks and carried out other duties as sentries and despatch riders. There were about 200 women and 200 men in the first 'mixed' battery.

Author's collection

Volunteers from the ATS began training with male recruits in the Anti-Aircraft Command during the spring of 1940. Hitherto regarded as all-male preserves, the prospect of 'mixed' batteries was regarded by old gunners as amusing and unorthodox. New recruits are shown here being introduced to an AA gun.

Author's collection

Young women of the ATS working with a sound-locator. After lengthy training, they proved steady in action and certainly the equal of men in their allotted tasks, although they did not undertake the heavy work of firing the guns. The first German aircraft known to have been shot down by a mixed battery crashed near Newcastle-on-Tyne on 8 December 1941.

Author's collection

By 8 October 1940, a month after the Blitz against London began, this unnamed factory employing 1,200 people in the Docklands area had been hit on eight occasions. It was continuing to function, with smelters still at work while a crater from a bomb which had crashed through the roof was being filled up.

Author's collection

Carbon-arc 90cm searchlights, providing 210 million candle-power, were used to probe the night sky during the Blitz against Britain.

Author's collection

Oberleutnant Vogt, Staffelkäpitan of
4./Jagdgeschwader 3, after rescue from the
Channel on 8 October 1940. He ditched his
Messerschmitt Bf109E-4 after it had been badly
damaged by RAF fighters during a sortie over
London.

Bruce Robertson collection

King George VI on a visit to a Bomber Command station, examining maps in the Operations Room. Air Marshal Sir Richard Peirse, the Air Officer Commanding-in-Chief of Bomber Command from 5 October 1940, is on the left. Air Vice-Marshal J.E.A. Baldwin, the Air Officer Commanding-in-Chief of No. 3 Group from August 1939, is on the right.
Author's collection

(*Left*) A Canadian air gunner in the RAF, sitting in the rear turret of an Armstrong Whitworth Whitley, displays the hole in his helmet made by a piece of flak fired during one of his trips over Germany.
Author's collection

(*Overleaf*) German aircraft, shot down by fighters or anti-aircraft fire, collected at a dump in an RAF station. Identifiable are the fuselage of a Junkers Ju87 Stuka, the fuselages of two Dornier DO17Z-2s and part of the tail fin of another Do17Z-2.
Author's collection

Luftwaffe prisoners passing through London under armed escort. Some had been provided with sports jackets, presumably having lost part of their uniforms when being shot down.

Author's collection

A batch of Luftwaffe prisoners, shot down in the Battle of Britain, being taken by coach to prisoner-of-war camp.

Author's collection

A wounded Luftwaffe prisoner arriving at a London terminus under armed escort, walking with the aid of a stick and with his few possessions in a carrier bag.

Author's collection

Firemen tackling a 30ft pillar of flame from a ruptured gas main in a London street after a night raid. The asphalt in the street and the houses on the right are also ablaze.

Author's collection

Men of the Pioneer Corps were called in to
start clearing up some of the bomb damage in
the Blitz.

Author's collection

The King talking to firemen in the dockland area
of London which had suffered air raid damage.

Author's collection

The Queen chatting to women and children during a tour of South London to inspect air raid damage.

Author's collection

A 4.5in anti-aircraft gun of Western Command
in action at night.

Author's collection

Some of the heavy anti-aircraft guns which arrived from factories and other parts of the country to encircle London when the Blitz against the capital began during the Battle of Britain.

Author's collection

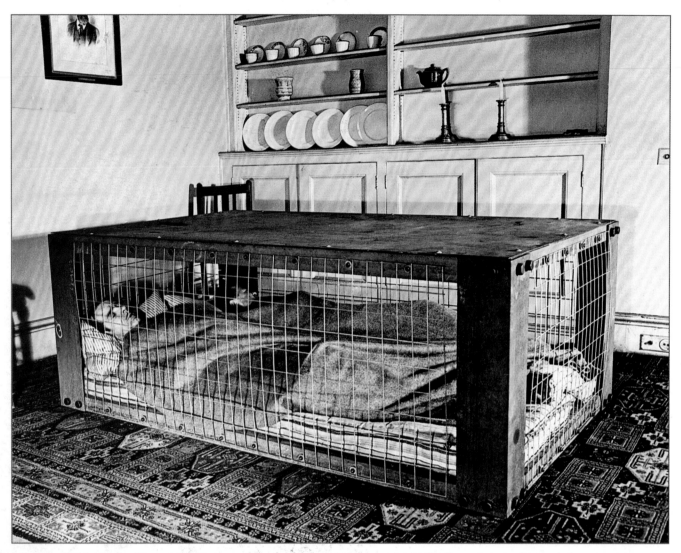

A new indoor 'table' shelter was demonstrated in the House of Commons for those who had to remain inside their houses during bombing attacks. It was named the 'Morrison shelter' after the Home Secretary, Herbert Morrison.

Author's collection

Pilot Officer Thomas F. Neil flew Hurricane Is of 249 Squadron during the Battle of Britain. He was awarded a Distinguished Flying Cross in October 1940, when he had been credited with five victories and two shared. He later received a Bar after being credited with two more. This photograph shows him as a flight lieutenant chatting to Mary Stanyer at work, when he visited a cotton mill in Oldham which made airmen's clothes. He is reported as having told the mill girls: 'When this war is finished the men in the services will have fought in it – but you will have won it.'

Author's collection

The RAF's first four-engined bomber, the Short Stirling, was being built during the Battle of Britain. No. 7 Squadron at Leeming in Yorkshire was the first to receive the new aircraft, in August 1940, but operational sorties did not begin until the night of 10/11 February 1941.

Author's collection

The ill-starred Avro Manchester was in production during the Battle of Britain but did not enter squadron service until November 1940. With two Rolls-Royce Vulture engines of 1,760hp, it was underpowered and also suffered from engine failures. It was withdrawn from front-line service in June 1942, but had the merit of being the forerunner of the highly successful Avro Lancaster four-engined bomber. This Manchester I serial L7427 was on the strength of 83 Squadron based at Scampton, Lincs.

Author's collection

A British lance corporal examining the fuselage of Messerschmitt Bf109E-1, works number 3576 of 7./Jagdgeschwader 54 'Grünherz'. This aircraft was flown by Unteroffizier Arno Zimmermann on 27 October 1940 during a fighter sweep over the Kent area. It was attacked and severely damaged by RAF fighters and Zimmermann was forced to make a belly-landing near Lydd marshes. He was captured unhurt.

Philip Jarrett collection

The victory in the Battle of Britain inspired Captain Henry Broughton of Engelfield Green, Surrey, who presented this Hurricane I serial V7773 to the RAF. It was named 'Surrey' and first entered RAF service with No. 10 Maintenance Unit on 6 December 1940, before being crated and shipped to Takoradi in the Gold Coast. Machines were assembled at this sea terminus and flown to Egypt for service in the Western Desert.

Bruce Robertson collection

The RAF received a welcome present on 27 November 1940 when this Messerschmitt Bf109E-4 of 2./Jagdgeschwader 51 'Mölders', flown by Leutnant Wolfgang Teumer, force-landed at Manston in Kent after an air battle with Spitfires. With RAF livery and the serial number DG200, it could be flown in mock combat with Hurricanes and Spitfires to assess the relative strengths and weaknesses of each type of fighter. This aircraft is now on display at the RAF Museum in Hendon.

Philip Jarrett collection

On 11 November 1940 ten Fiat BR20 bombers of 43° Stormo, escorted by forty CR42S of 18° Gruppo, took off from the Belgian bases of Chievres and Maldegem for a raid on Harwich Harbour. The Italian force was attacked by Hurricanes, which shot down three bombers and three fighters, and damaged others. The surviving aircraft landed at various bases. This BR20M of 243° Squadriglia, 99° Gruppo, crashed into the fir trees of Tangham Forest in Suffolk. Two crew members were killed and four taken prisoner. The insignia had been cut from the fins when this photograph was taken.

Philip Jarrett collection

A line-up of Hurricanes and Spitfires on 18 April 1968 at RAF Henlow in Bedfordshire. It had taken three years to gather these aircraft and eighteen months to make them serviceable for the film *The Battle of Britain*. Wing Commander Robert Stanford-Tuck, who had ten victories to his credit and was acting as tactical adviser for the British side of the film, was photographed standing beside the Hurricane in the foreground. The German side was filmed in Spain.

Aeroplane

Sergeant John Stanley Gilders flew with 72 Squadron and then with 616 Squadron in the Battle of Britain before joining 41 Squadron in November 1940. On 21 February 1941 he took off in Spitfire IIA serial 7816 from Hornchurch as one of a patrol of six aircraft. The formation was at 32,000ft when he turned steeply and dived to earth, probably from oxygen failure. The Spitfire crashed on a farm near Chilham in Kent, exploding and forming a crater about 16ft deep, which rapidly filled with water. Pieces of the aircraft were recovered by No. 49 Maintenance Group but John Gilders' body was not found.

On 20 April 1994 a team of amateur aviation archaeologists led by Mark A. Kirby excavated the site of the crash and recovered the remains of the body. A military funeral took place at Brookwood Military Cemetery on 11 May 1995, with pall bearers from the RAF Regiment and members of John Gilders' family in attendance.

Mark A. Kirby

The Battle of Britain Memorial at Capel-le-Ferne, Dover, Kent. This memorial was conceived by Wing Commander A. Geoffrey Page, DSO, OBE, DFC*, who served in 56 Squadron. On 12 August 1940, when a Pilot Officer, his Hurricane serial P2970 from North Weald in Essex was shot down during an attack on Dornier Do17s of Kampfgeschwader 2. He baled out into the sea 10 miles north of Margate in Kent, and was picked up badly burnt.

Dover District Council agreed to lease for a peppercorn rent a 7 acre site on the cliff top to a Trust which was formed. Many companies and individuals contributed to the Trust. The Carving Workshop at Cambridge, with landscape architect Jamie Buchanan, worked on the project. The central figure is a young pilot looking out over the Channel, seated on a sandstone plinth on which are carved the crests of all the squadrons which participated in the Battle. The Queen Mother unveiled the Memorial on 9 July 1992.

Knowler Edmonds collection

The statue of Air Chief Marshal Lord Dowding outside St Clement Danes, the Royal Air Force Church in Aldwych, London. It was unveiled by the Queen Mother on Sunday 30 October 1988, in the presence of many Battle of Britain pilots. A Guard of Honour from the Queen's Colour Squadron presented arms while the Royal Air Force Central Band played the National Anthem.

Author's collection

SELECT
BIBLIOGRAPHY

Andrews, Allen, *The Air Marshals*, London: Macdonald, 1970.

Bowyer, Michael J.F., *The Battle of Britain 50 Years On*, Wellingborough: Patrick Stephens, 1990.

Chant, Christopher, *Warfare and the Third Reich*, London: Salamander, 1996.

Collier, Basil, *Leader of the Few*, London: Jarrolds, 1957.

——, *The Defence of the United Kingdom*, London: HMSO, 1957.

De Decker, Cynrik & Roba, Jean-Louis, *Mei 1940 boven België*, Erembodegem: Uitgeverij de Krijger, 1993.

Deighton, Len, *Fighter*, London: Triad Granada, 1979.

Ellis, L.F., *The War in France and Flanders*, London: HMSO, 1953.

Forty, George & Duncan, John, *The Fall of France*, London: Guild, 1990.

Gahyde, Yvon, *L'Attaque Aérienne des Ponts du Canal Albert*, Service Historique des Forces Armées, 1980.

Galland, Adolf, *The First and the Last*, London: Methuen, 1955.

Hindley, F.H. et al., *British Intelligence in the Second World War, Volume 1*, London: HMSO, 1979.

Homze, Edward L., *Arming the Luftwaffe*, Lincoln: University of Nebraska Press, 1976.

Ishoven, Armand van, *The Luftwaffe and the Battle of Britain*, Shepperton: Ian Allan, 1980.

Mason, Francis K., *The Hawker Hurricane*, Bourne End: Aston Publications, 1987.

Mitcham, Samuel W., *Eagles of the Third Reich*, London: Guild, 1989.

Price, Alfred, *The Hardest Day*, London: Cassell, 1998.

Probert, Henry & Cox, Sebastian, *The Battle Re-Thought*, Shrewsbury: Airlife, 1991.

Public Record Office:

    AIR 41/15 *The Air Defence of Great Britain, Volume II. The Battle of Britain*.

    AIR 41/16 *Appendices and maps*.

    CAB 106/1206 War Cabinet Historical Section. *Correspondence with Basil Collier*.

Ramsey, Winston G., *The Battle of Britain Then and Now*, London: After the Battle, 1982.

——, *The Blitz Then and Now, Volume 2*. London: After the Battle, 1988.

Ray, John, *The Battle of Britain: New Perspectives*, London: Arms & Armour, 1994.

Richards, Denis, *Royal Air Force 1939–1945, Volume 1*, London: HMSO, 1953.

Ritchie, Sebastian, *Industry and Air Power*, London: Frank Cass, 1997.

Roskill, S.W., *The War at Sea, Volume 1*, London: HMSO, 1954.

Snyder, Louis L., *Encyclopedia of the Third Reich*, London: Blandford, 1989.

Toliver, Raymond F. & Constable, Trevor J., *Fighter Aces of the Luftwaffe*, Fallbrook: Aero, 1977.

——, *Fighter General – The Life of Adolf Galland*, Zephyr Cove: AmPress, 1990.

Wood, Derek & Dempster, Derek, *The Narrow Margin*, London: Tri-Service Press, 1990.

Wright, Robert, *Dowding and the Battle of Britain*, London: Macdonald, 1969.

INDEX